In Celebration of Print.

Hubert Graf

First published in the United States of America in 1997 by

UNIVERSE PUBLISHING

A Division of Rizzoli International Publications, Inc.

300 Park Avenue South, New York, NY 10010

97 98 99/ 10 9 8 7 6 5 4 3 2 1

Printed in Italy

Catalog Card Number: 97-60146

The work of Hubert Graf is not for idle viewing, although the viewing in itself is a rich experience. This is a body of work to be studied and absorbed in all its multi-layered dimensions. It will bring one to the realization that print advertising, when generated from the mind and hand of a classicist, can indeed become an art form. An art form with commercial purpose. One that connects with the reader at a level of intelligence and respect seldom attained, much less maintained, in the selling of goods and services.

The subtle, powerful magnetism of Hubert Graf's work surfaces in an illustration that transcends a mere drawing. A photograph that stirs the senses. Color that carries a message. A type face so relevant it strengthens the word. And white space. A tool vastly misunderstood and often misused, even by skilled art directors. Here, white space empowers the elements surrounding it, forming a challenge to even the casual reader, "Just try to skip this page."

Even more than the visual impact, the emotional impact of Hubert Graf's work is resounding. Readers are confronted, not with the usual product hype, but rather with a thought-provoking dialogue that addresses their personal needs, wants... and yes, even fantasies.

In this age of accelerating change, intellectual preoccupation with technology, headlong thrust into globalization with attendant cultural upheavals, work grounded in timeless basics brings great value to the task of universal communication. No trendy techniques here, no mere work of the times. Rather, work that is helping define the times. As effective today as yesterday, as effective tomorrow as today.

Having worked with Hubert, though not nearly often enough, I early came to appreciate the sparks he gives off, along with his innate ability to finish your thought. Often, very often, elevating it to another level.

Saluté, Hubert.

Jim Durfee

As we embrace the digital age, print advertising becomes more relevant than ever. Despite the promise of the "paperless office," improvements in printing, facsimile, and reproductive technology create an insatiable demand for more, not less, paper-based media. This, in turn, creates more opportunities for communication through print advertising.

As more data and information comes on line, the importance of the craft increases proportionately to the tonnage of generic information produced.

The unfortunate reality is that many of the architects of the increased volume of print are technicians driven by the technological possibilities of the medium rather than the necessities of the marketplace. The result? More "data" that makes no connection with the reader – that slips by unnoticed; more generic information that is not transformed into useful knowledge. And yet knowledge is the essential conduit between supply and demand. If today's communication is to fulfill its original purpose of serving the needs of both the advertiser and the reader, it requires the added value of creativity. Only then is a bridge to the customer really created. Cynics feel that this process amounts to manipulation, but the creative translation of raw data is not manipulative; rather, at its best it is a concise, if subjective, presentation that simultaneously informs and entertains.

The goal of effective advertising is to establish a one-on-one relationship between the advertiser and the reader through the use of verbal and visual metaphors that communicate the character and attributes not only of the featured product or services, but also of the sponsor, the brand. How the information is conveyed establishes the personality of the brand and eventually accumulates into the much sought after brand equity. Balancing these components may appear deceptively simple; creating the ad, however, is a sophisticated art.

Crafting communication must be driven by the audience to whom it is directed. It must be for their benefit and their benefit only. So communication is only as successful as the reaction it elicits. The challenge is to translate what is, in some cases, a rather mundane message into a motivating, often visceral response. This process attracts a very specific type of person. It offers the constant challenge of leveraging energy to achieve either a brilliant or a mediocre result. Thus, the near epic struggle of the creator is often as intense as the feeling of relief when the solution is born. Of course, the process of arriving at "the big idea" takes not just inspiration but a well- thought-out strategy, product knowledge, and research intelligence from the customer's point of view. But at the end of the day, it is still that singular effort, that moment of truth which prevails. The creative process is nothing if not individualistic.

Strategies may vary from one client to the next, but the principles used to build effective communication remain constant. Especially as the metaphorical language eliminates geographical borders and the demographics of the global audience grow increasingly similar. This lets brand assets flow freely through all channels of international commerce. Many businesses are finally, and somewhat reluctantly, coming to this conclusion. And the race is on.

The necessity to differentiate, to break the parity that exists between so many brands, has become crucial. And effective communication that delivers short-range incremental values is an attractive alternative to long-range capital investments. The response from the marketplace is as reliable as the echo: the quality of the response is in direct correlation to the quality of the initial communication. This "real time" playback is essential intelligence for a sponsor and serves as a litmus test for the spreadsheet assumptions of their forecasters. In this way, the customer also participates in building the corporate strategy – a reality check to remind the sponsor of its reliance on the marketplace. As Bill Bernbach, one of the giants of advertising, so succinctly put it, "Nothing kills a bad product faster than good advertising."

And nothing makes a good product more successful than brilliant advertising. It adds value to the product and creates higher perceptions and thus higher expectations, which in turn forces the producers to live up to their promises. Perception then becomes reality for the customer.

The responsibility of the producer of communication is to three constituencies: the sponsor, the audience, himself. It is to communicate value that would otherwise remain obscure, and thus making communication an inseparable part of any product or service. It is also to remind the unaware that communication, as qualitative as it is, can often prove to be even more valuable as a quantifiable fixed asset.

Hubert Graf

INTRODUCING THE NEW SWISSAIR BUSINESS CLASS FOR EUROPE. CONSIDERING HOW WE TREAT YOU FROM TOP TO BOTTOM, YOU'LL FALL IN LOVE WITH US HEAD OVER HEELS.

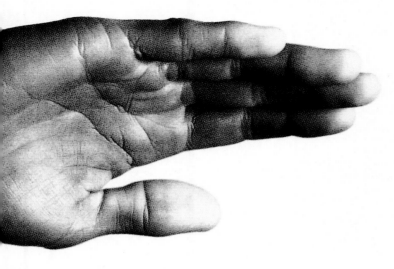
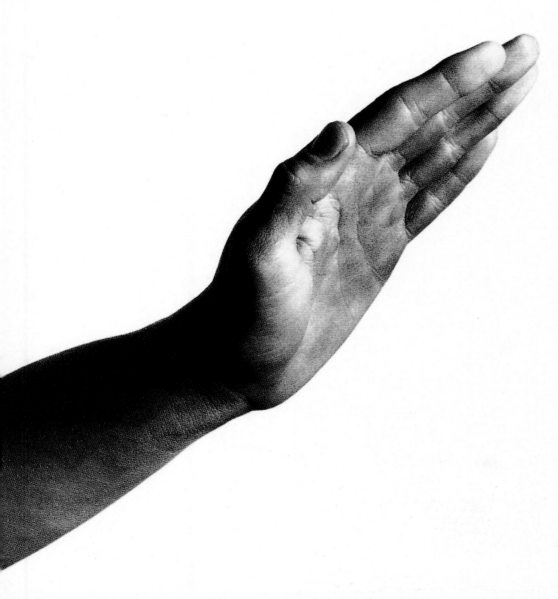

business ✚

Because of their long-standing reputation for customer service, **Swissair** is the last of the major commercial airlines within continental Europe to change their seating configuration from three classes to the now widely accepted choices of economy and business.

While other airlines' ads emphasize that their new business class is as good as their old first class, Swissair approaches the problem from a different perspective.

They position their business class as a totally new and proprietary category, thereby creating a new benchmark for service, and immediately separating themselves from the competition.

The campaign itself is an example of how to effectively leverage brand equity by demonstrating an appreciation and understanding of exactly what the business traveler's expectations are: the liberation from the drudgery of today's air travel.

Hence, the metaphor of the "flying man."

The campaign consists of seven ads, each with a portion of the flying man image and a message.

Every week one more is revealed, creating mystery, suspense, and yes, some aggravation, culminating in the crescendo and revelation – the complete figure.

Photography by Albert Watson lends the campaign an element of fashion and lifestyle not previously associated with the airline business.

In order to diverge from a traditional format, the copy is handwritten and the logo is left out until the final frame, giving the ad the appearance of an editorial. This highly charged aesthetic is juxtaposed with simple, cut-and-dried copy stating the most elementary physical benefits of the business class.

As a result, the metaphor of the "Renaissance Man" performs his duty, and Swissair quickly climbs to the top of the charts.

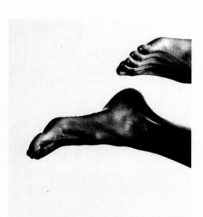

ON MARCH 28, SWISSAIR TAKES AN IMPORTANT STEP FORWARD; IN EUROPE, WE'LL COMBINE FIRST AND BUSINESS AND TURN IT INTO THE NEW SWISSAIR BUSINESS CLASS FOR EUROPE.

YOUR LEGS ARE LOOKING FORWARD TO MARCH 28 AND THE NEW SWISSAIR BUSINESS CLASS FOR EUROPE. YOU'LL BE A STEP AHEAD AT CHECK-IN AND BAGGAGE CLAIM.

YOUR KNEES ARE LOOKING FORWARD TO MARCH 28 AND THE NEW SPACIOUS SWISSAIR BUSINESS CLASS FOR EUROPE. MOVE YOUR KNEES FROM SIDE TO SIDE – THEY'LL DISCOVER MORE ROOM, MORE FREEDOM. AND WHEN YOU CROSS YOUR LEGS, YOU WON'T MAKE THE PERSON NEXT TO YOU CROSS.

THE MUSCLES YOU SIT ON ARE LOOKING FORWARD TO MARCH 28 AND THE FIRST CONTACT WITH THE NEW SWISSAIR BUSINESS CLASS FOR EUROPE. AND OUR RUMBOLD SEAT, DESIGNED WITH ERGONOMICS IN MIND, CALLS FOR A SITTING OVATION.

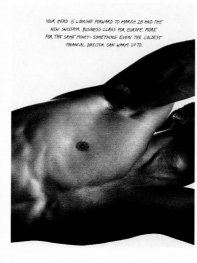

YOUR STOMACH IS LOOKING FORWARD TO MARCH 28 AND
THE NEW SWISSAIR BUSINESS CLASS FOR EUROPE. EVEN ON THE
SHORTEST OF SHORT-HAUL FLIGHTS, YOU'LL FIND A
WELCOME DINING SURPRISE. OUR NEW CUISINE WILL GIVE
OTHER AIRLINES SOME FOOD FOR THOUGHT.

YOUR HEAD IS LOOKING FORWARD TO MARCH 28 AND THE
NEW SWISSAIR BUSINESS CLASS FOR EUROPE. MORE
FOR THE SAME MONEY— SOMETHING EVEN THE COLDEST
FINANCIAL DIRECTOR CAN WARM UP TO.

INTRODUCING THE NEW SWISSAIR BUSINESS CLASS FOR
EUROPE. CONSIDERING HOW WE TREAT YOU FROM TOP TO BOTTOM, YOU'LL
FALL IN LOVE WITH US HEAD OVER HEELS.

business

Flying the colors of **Swissair**
business class is a silk scarf
produced in India and adorned
with the "flying man" and a poem
by St. Exupery, the illustrious
French writer and philosopher
who also happened to be an
aviator. Like St. Exupery,
the flying man takes the art of
flying into spiritual heights,
in effect, becoming the logo for
the business class, appearing
everywhere the Swissair
business class goes to and
comes from: from a ten-second
commercial to a brooch on the
blouse of a flight attendant to
a t-shirt or a matchbook.
This synergy is not only
aesthetically pleasing, it is a
requirement in order to build
a hard-working horizontal
nomenclature.
The scarf was arbitrarily
distributed to the flying staff
and customers, creating an
artificial scarcity, enhancing
interest in the product and
notoriety for the brand.

SOMETIMES THE STRANGEST JUXTAPOSITIONS JUST HAPPEN.

Equinox Bowl by Neil Cohen. Width 9½″, $385. Catalogue $5. Fifth Avenue at 56th Street, New York, NY 10022. 212 752-1441.

STEUBEN
THE CLEAREST FORM OF EXPRESSION

An all-too-familiar marketing dilemma: a brand, in this case **Steuben**, has come to rely too heavily on an aging and shrinking customer base. They need to reach the younger end of the affluent market and compete for their disposable income with many other appealing luxury items, from watches and jewelry to exotic vacations and art. While aiming for a younger market, it is nevertheless essential that the company not alienate the existing customer base who will continue to provide the revenue stream essential for the growth of Steuben. Before developing the new campaign, extensive research in the form of focus groups was conducted in various parts of the country. By studying the attitudinal responses of the group members, a final campaign is developed to blend a dramatic, at times surreal, imagery that maintains the product as a centerpiece even with the obligatory pricepoint. The campaign is appealing to the younger members of the target audience. They begin to see Steuben in a new light reinforced by the tagline, "The Clearest Form of Expression." They can, for the first time, picture themselves owning a "Steuben." And since the ads reflect the buyers' sophisticated taste, the traditional audience can confirm their loyalty to Steuben.

This is a classic repositioning of an illustrious and venerable brand.

Part of Corning since 1918. © Corning 1988

STEUBEN
THE CLEAREST FORM OF EXPRESSION

Part of Corning since 1918. © Corning 1989

STEUBEN
THE CLEAREST FORM OF EXPRESSION

Steuben wishes to remind its
audience of the unique quality
and intrinsic value of every
piece that bears its name.
How better to achieve this
than by celebrating its artisans
through a campaign.
The integrity, quality, and
preciousness of the crystal
and its design is emphasized
by presenting the object with
its creator.
The artists are, in turn,
portrayed by another artist,
the photographer Irving Penn.
Penn's photographs depict the
artists in the spirit of crystal and
crystal-making, in striking black
and white. Penn portrays the
artists through absolute
precision, absolute clarity, not
embellished by color.
By presenting Steuben as the
work of contemporary artists,
its perception is elevated.
Steuben the utility becomes
Steuben the art.

As the venerable supplier
of gifts for the White House
to give to heads of state,
Steuben presents its collection
for the first time in the *Wall
Street Journal*.
The ad presents a selection
of Steuben's extensive
inventory, artistic as well as
functional pieces.
It addresses companies who
wish to extend Steuben as a
prestigious momento reserved
not only for heads of state,
but for corporations and their
employees as well.
This is an example of how
an ad can sell a product and
at the same time support
the prestige of the brand.

Handkerchief Vase, 8618n, Width 9 1/2", $625

Trout & Fly, 1002n, Height 8", $2,150

Dervish Vase, 8598n, Height 6", $950

Whirlpool Vase, 8087n, Height 11", $875

Eagle, 8130n, Wingspread 12", $740

Ram's Head Candy Dish, 7936n, Height 5", $640

Cut Paperweight with Teardrop, 1039n, Height 3 1/4", $1,295

Floating Spheres, 8401n, Height 2", $260

Close to the Wind, 1068n, Height 8", $4,200

Heritage Flared Vase, 7706n, Height 9 3/8", $695

Eagle, 8496n, Height 3 3/8", $340

Hellenic Urn, 8592n, Height 9 1/2", $900

Saturn Paperweight, 8609n, Diameter approx. 5 1/2", $475

Shooting Star, 1130n, Height 5", $1,750

Elephant, 8128n, Height 7 1/2", $825

Horse Head, 7779n, Height 5", $310

Excalibur, 1000n, Height 8", $3,100

1992 Crystal, 8624n, Height 2 1/2", $295

An American tradition for
nearly ninety years, a gift of
Steuben is perhaps the most
eloquent holiday statement one
could make without uttering a
single word. For information
about our special corporate services or to request our corporate
catalogue, call 800 424-4240.
Or visit our Fifth Avenue store at
56th Street in New York City.

STEUBEN

What differentiates one hotel
from another is not its features
as much as its location and
brand perception. The "Swiss"
in **Swissôtel** reminds the
sophisticated reader of quality,
attention to detail, and hospitality. In this case, the reader's
preconceived notion of "Swiss"
is translated into a product and
brand differentiation.
The visual metaphor of
"singular identity" makes
the point.
Since Swissôtels vary in
category, and are a
combination of partly
managed and partly owned
properties all over the world,
it is essential to build a single
brand image which overrides
all differences.
The fact that all Swissôtels
can stand under one umbrella
image not only delivers
attractive economic rewards,
but is also essential for building
the all-important brand equity.

There are hotels and there is Swissôtel.

Is one hotel beginning to look like another to you? Then experience the fine art of Swissôtel. Every hotel is centrally located to business. Attention to service is a way of life. Spacious rooms are the norm. All complimented by exquisite cuisine. Swissôtel, one of a kind, with properties in New York, Boston, Chicago and opening early 1991, Atlanta - Buckhead. Because if the Swiss can't run a hotel, who can? Call 800-63-SWISS for reservations.

swissôtel

NEW YORK
THE DRAKE HOTEL

swissôtel

BOSTON
THE LAFAYETTE HOTEL

swissôtel

CHICAGO

swissôtel

ATLANTA

Swissôtel does not discount room rates or offer free extra nights – both cannibalize precious yield. Instead, the hotels capitalize on their Swiss origin by offering a gram of pure gold for each night of occupancy. The sum total of each night's stay accumulates into a gold bar issued, of course, by Credit Suisse. Uniquely Swiss, this promotion is also extremely cost-effective because the price of a gram of gold is far less than the more obvious, generic incentive of free rooms.

There are rewards and there is Swissôtel.

Are all hotel frequent traveler programs beginning to look the same to you? Then come to Swissôtel where frequent guests are rewarded with, not points, not free rooms, but solid gold. Solid gold bars from Credit Suisse. Stay as few as ten nights in any Swissôtel in the U.S and get the gold. It's that simple.

Only the roads to Swissôtel are paved with gold. They are in New York, Boston, Chicago and, opening early 1991, Atlanta Buckhead.

To learn more about the Swissôtel Gold Account™ call 800 63-SWISS.

swissôtel
NEW YORK
THE DRAKE HOTEL

swissôtel
BOSTON
THE LAFAYETTE HOTEL

swissôtel
CHICAGO

swissôtel
ATLANTA

This full-page newspaper
ad ran only once – tactically in
tandem with the same ad in
magazines. It was a gamble
considering the cost of a
national *Wall Street Journal* ad.
However, it was worth the risk.
This "wanted" ad rallied the
target profile, the readers
of the *Wall Street Journal*,
to join. The response was
overwhelming: close to 5,000
readers signed up.
Swissôtel not only increased
its occupancy but also
gained a brand new set of
repeat customers.

Gold.

Only at Swissôtel can you strike Gold in your sleep. Solid Gold from Credit Suisse. Just for being a member of the Swissôtel Gold Account and staying as few as ten nights (not necessarily consecutive), you'll get a 5 gram bar of Gold. Stay more nights, get more Gold. It's that easy.

Now striking it rich is even easier. From March 19 through May 31, 1991 you can receive an extra credit toward getting the Gold. To get your bonus credit, as well as instant membership, just present this coupon at check out or mail it to the address below. And do hurry, you know what happened the last time word leaked out about a Gold Rush.

For information and reservations call 800-63-SWISS.

Swissôtel Gold Account Program
440 Park Avenue
New York, NY 10022

Name _____ Tel # (___) _____

Mailing Address _____

City _____ State ____ Zip _____

Limit one coupon per stay. Some rate restrictions apply. Offer good only in North America. Only original coupon valid.

Rush!

swissôtel
NEW YORK
THE DRAKE HOTEL

swissôtel
CHICAGO

swissôtel
ATLANTA

swissôtel
BOSTON
THE LAFAYETTE HOTEL

Since the nineteenth century, **Taittinger** champagne and its vintage cuveé, the "Comptes de Champagne," have been among the truly great classic champagnes. By using a kaleidoscopic collage of upper-class, blue-blood images, the campaign weaves a rich and evocative story, overwhelmingly romantic in its associations. Historic black-and-white images from the world-famous Magnum photography archives in Paris, in the style of Henri Cartier-Bresson (the renowned founder of Magnum), are used throughout the campaign. The photographs are arranged in such a way as to provide testimony to the sophisticated reputation of the Taittinger brand. Because the campaign unashamedly plays to the elite, it becomes a logical reflection of the status and quality of the product, a symbol of the lifestyle it represents.

TIMELESS...TAITTINGER. LEGACY OF THE COMTES DE CHAMPAGNE.

TIMELESS...TAITTINGER. LEGACY OF THE COMTES DE CHAMPAGNE.

TIMELESS…TAITTINGER. LEGACY OF THE COMTES DE CHAMPAGNE.

At the time of this ad campaign,
the **Aston Martin** Lagonda
was the most expensive, most
luxuriously appointed car of its
type in the world.
The ad plays on the status of the
Aston Martin Lagonda through
tongue-in-cheek humor and a
"loud" understatement. Placed
in the *Wall Street Journal* in
the eighties, the ad humorously
reflects the acquisitive
preoccupation of the decade.
It was chosen by Dow Jones as
an example of how best to
make use of its medium in
order to arrive at the desired
result – sales.
And sell it did. It sold its total
allocation for the U.S. of
eighteen cars. Not a big deal
by American standards,
but considering the price tag
of $250,000, it is a great
testimony to what a creative
approach in the proper
medium can do.

Demoralize thy neighbor.

It's one thing to trundle by in a Bentley, Jaguar, Mercedes or the like. Everyone in your neighborhood has one of those.

It's quite another thing to come in for a landing in your Lagonda.

The Lagonda is an Aston Martin and Aston Martin reflects your personal style: everyone knows that you have one, but no one knows exactly what it is. The Lagonda is, in fact, the automotive paradox.

For example, at a time when many cars are made largely by robots, the Lagonda is made entirely by hand. The aluminum body panels are hammered into shape, welded, sanded and finished with 23 coats of lacquer. (It has been said that looking at the finish of a Lagonda is like falling into a pool.) Even the engine is hand-made and signed by one of our four engine builders.

The paradox continues.

The Lagonda is powerful and fast. Should you wish to drive at one-fifth the speed of sound, this is the safest car in the world to do it in.

For all its power, handling capability, and advanced electronic instrumentation, the Lagonda is a remarkably reliable and essentially simple car.

We build the Lagonda at the rate of three a week. Twenty-four are designated for the United States market each year. That's about as fast and as many as we can manage.

Should your neighbors ask you, as you glide by, what kind of car the Lagonda is, by all means tell them. Should they ask where they can get one, tell them they probably can't.

That should do it.

Write for our brochure.

Aston Martin Lagonda, 342 W. Putnam Ave., Greenwich, CT 06830, (203) 629-8830

The **Aston Martin** Volante, the famous two-seater lionized by James Bond, is the ultimate motorcar. Photographed in industrial Long Island City, New York, a rough backdrop provides a vivid contrast to the automobile's outrageous luxury and status. It evokes a sweet notion of adventure and nostalgia for those who remember the original .007 – not incidentally, the target audience. Given Aston Martin's reputation, any technical argument selling the car's features is superfluous.

"We truly succeed if there is no attack and no transaction."

J.P. Morgan's key objective as a financial advisor and defense strategist is to forestall an unwelcome approach in the first place. Fully valued companies are rarely attacked or forced to restructure under pressure. So we work with you to find and implement measures that encourage a full valuation by the market of the company's stock. If a merger is to your advantage, we'll help you get the best price at the best terms. The point is, J.P. Morgan brings a relationship focus to a transaction-driven business, a philosophy that distinguishes us from other firms. We don't promote M&A transactions simply to generate fees, but offer objective financial advice that serves your best interests.

JPMorgan

Empty tombstone underscores a J.P. Morgan credo: we don't do deals just to generate fees. If a transaction isn't in a client's interests, we'll recommend against it.

At the time of disappearing
bank regulations in the U.S.,
when American banks are once
again allowed to deal in
securities, Morgan Guaranty,
the preeminent investment
bank, embarks on its future by
referring to its past. It starts
by renaming the firm
J.P. Morgan after its
founder, the esteemed banker
and classic American
entrepreneur. This amounts to
a signal of intent to the global
investment community, as well
as to another important
constituency, the J.P. Morgan
employees, emphasizing that
the only change is to focus on
the original credo: "To serve the
best. By being the best."

"J.P. Morgan is an international firm with a very important American business."

For over 125 years J.P. Morgan has put its clients' interests first, in a context of absolute confidentiality and objectivity.

J.P. Morgan was an international firm long before the integration of world financial markets. Over the last century we have established a presence in major financial centers everywhere, building the global resources and experience multinational clients need. Today, whether we're raising capital in London or investing funds in Tokyo, trading currencies in Frankfurt or restructuring assets in New York, J.P. Morgan draws on in-depth company and industry research generated by our 120 analysts worldwide, and minute-by-minute data from Morgan market-makers in each financial center. Our clients know the advice we offer and the solutions we structure come from a global perspective no other firm can match.

JPMorgan

"The techniques change. The principles don't."

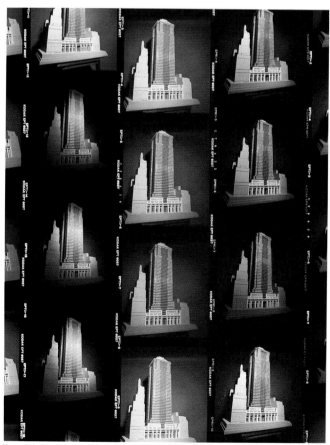

Change linked to continuity: J.P. Morgan's new headquarters rise on Wall Street two blocks from where the firm has had its principal offices for more than a century.

Combining capital strength with global financing, advisory, treasury, and investment skills, J.P. Morgan continues to innovate to serve our clients better. Yet the principles that guide us in today's integrated, technology-driven financial markets haven't changed in 125 years.

In everything we do we put the client's interests first, a way of doing business that produces impartial, objective advice on any matter, however confidential. Many years ago J.P. Morgan himself said it best: "The client's belief in the integrity of our advice is our best possession."

JPMorgan

J.P. Morgan has a sterling image as a blue chip investment bank. It is also innovative in that it provides the most complex financial engineering for institutional investors. The illustration for this ad comes from the actual notes scribbled during a meeting by one of Morgan's senior bankers. This gives the ad a sense of immediacy and authenticity, both important facets of the decision-making process involved in managing huge pension funds.

"The benefits of diversifying are clear. But who can show you all the possibilities?"

Diversification can reduce your exposure to risk. It can add value to your plan. But diversifying successfully is easier said than done.

At J.P.Morgan Investment Management, we can help you take a comprehensive overview of all the possibilities. Drawing on the breadth and depth of our global organization, we can address all your questions and help you evaluate the implications of every course of action:"should international fixed-income assets be added?":"which hedging strategies should be considered?:"can I take advantage of rising markets without being hurt by volatile currencies?"

Even if your relationship with Morgan is based on just one of our many capabilities, you'll find us willing and able to share our global expertise in meeting every investment challenge.

To know more about our broad base of resources, and our commitment to building long-term relationships, please call or write John Thomas, Managing Director, 522 Fifth Avenue, New York, NY 10036. (212) 837-4424.

JPMorgan Investment Management

Some of Our Non-Traditional Investment Capabilities

Convertibles
Oil and gas
Real estate
International dollar and non-dollar
Small company stocks
Private placements
Derivative securities

JPMorgan

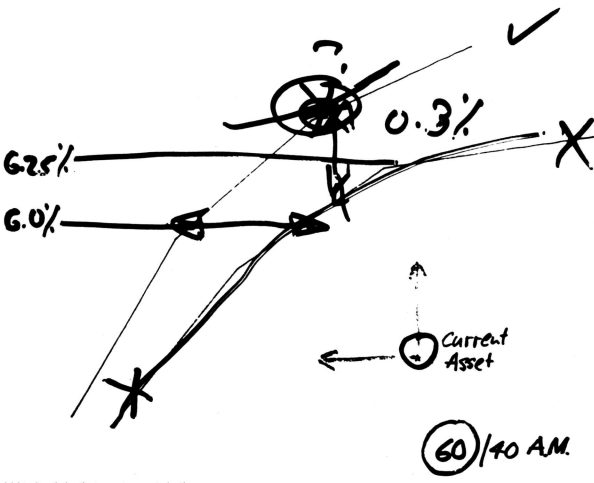

In helping clients plot diversification strategies, we examine the widest possible range of alternatives, with a preference for those that enhance long-term return without increasing risk.

Swissair counts on a reliable
constituency of affluent,
informed travelers who
have a positive opinion of
the airline. However, the
knowledge that Swissair flies
to destinations other than
Switzerland (more than 120
in sixty-four countries) and is,
in fact, a global airline,
is limited. Satisfied with
its firmly established reputation,
leveraging its perception as
one of the world's best airlines,
Swissair wanted this campaign
to enhance its association with
worldwide destinations.
The ads present an array of
visuals that depict Swissair
destinations. The only, but
essential, copy reference is the
visual mechanism of the red
timetable consistently placed
in each ad. Small captions
running vertically up the side
reveal the destination.
In this case, "Destination 74:
Munich." It is, of course, a luxury
to say nothing more, and in this
case the brand awareness is such
that a mere signal suffices.
No hard-selling necessary.
The sophisticated imagery
reflects the value and lifestyle
of the aspiring customer with
an approach that is a classic
example of "selling up."
The potential customers would
like to be associated with an
airline that had this type of
image, and the existing
customers feel confirmed
in their choice.

Destination No. 10: Barcelona.   Swissair. The civilized way to the world.®

As a traditional European vacation destination, **Switzerland** can present itself in one of two ways: it can follow the stereotypes, or fight them. A typical dilemma. Does one emphasize what one is already known for or attempt to change how one is perceived? Switzerland is seen as a country of breathtaking natural beauty. In itself, this is a rather generic description. But, if this concept is taken one step further to include broader cultural distinctions such as Switzerland's high standard of service and its sophisticated infrastructure, it establishes the uniqueness of Switzerland in general, and as a vacation destination, in particular. So, back to the future. The visuals feature timeless nature photography of archetypal Swiss landscapes, images evoking an environment and its evolution; the basic qualities of tranquil beauty and appreciation of nature that are sought after in any decade. The bold, "stamped" headline is in such dramatic contrast to the romantic images that it garners equal attention without interfering with the landscapes.

FÜR LEIB UND SEELE.

Stirn und Arme kühlen im Wasser, das eiskalt aus der Brunnenröhre schiesst. Dem Wind lauschen, wenn er durchs Gras und um die Baumwipfel streicht. In ein Bad gleiten, das mit seiner Kraft aus den Tiefen der Berge Schönheit und Wohlbefinden schenkt. Im spiegelnden See das Blau des Himmels und das Weiss der Wolken sehen und wiedersehen. Sich auf ein Menu voller Surprises freuen, den Abend beim freundschaftlichen Gespräch ausklingen lassen.

Und morgen weiter eintauchen in die fast uferlose Vielfalt der Schweiz.

Endlich Ferien. Ihre Schweiz.

IN DER BLAUEN LAGUNE.

Eine leise Ahnung von Meer und in der Luft der süsse Duft von Oleander. Weisse Segel, die über Seen gleiten, in denen sich erst Gipfel mit ewigem Schnee, dann weite Ebenen und hohe Wolken spiegeln. Bäche, die über Felsen und durch Wiesen voller Bergblumen rauschen. Noch lange am sonnenwarmen Steintisch unter funkelnden Sternen sitzen.

Und träumen von der Entdeckung der ganzen Vielfalt und Schönheit der Schweiz.

Endlich Ferien. Ihre Schweiz.

VON NATUR AUS SCHÖPFERISCH.

Romantische Streichquartette, die aus der offenen Tür einer

Kapelle wehen. Der Alpsegen, der von der Fluh herab

den Abend grüsst. Junge Texte, vorgetragen an sommerlich

warmen Literaturtagen. Jazz- und Rockmusik, die unter

freiem Himmel die Open air aufheizt. Und fürs Auge barocke

Kirchen, historische Stadtbilder und Formen modernster

Architektur. Filmfestivals, Kunsthallen und Museen:

Vielschichtig und tief verwurzelt ist die Kultur im

Ferienland Schweiz.

Endlich Ferien. Ihre Schweiz.

The perception of a product
or service, negative or positive,
represents energy that
communication can leverage.
As this relates to the three
examples shown from the
Swissair 'windows' campaign,
we had the luxury of reinforcing
a perception that Switzerland
and Swissair are known for:
sophistication in extending
hospitality and conservatism
in spending and managing
money.
The repetition and frequency
of the aircraft windows in the
media produced the
cumulative effect of "Oh yes,
another Swissair window."
This campaign could have gone
on forever. It did not.

Swissair First Class.

Quite possibly the best. Anywhere.

Europe. Africa. Middle East. Far East. North and South America. *swissair* +

Swissair Business Class.

Comfort is the bottom line.

Europe. Africa. Middle East. Far East. North and South America. **swissair** +

The liquor industry has come up
with yet another new product,
Alizé, a combination of fine
cognac and passion-fruit juice.
As the subject of "Le Scandale,"
the analogy is, of course,
Alizé's association with that
other risqué situation,
the ménage à trois.
The older man represents
the cognac, the younger the
passion-fruit, and the woman
is the arbitrator and center
of attention.
N'est-ce pas?
The objective of the producers
was, naturally, to sell more
cognac to a new and younger
audience, notorious for
mixing liquor with every
imaginable liquid.
The concept parodies the
assumptions Americans have
about the French – that they are
hedonists who know how to
enjoy life (and to drink).
The scandalous merchandising
of this product in the liquor
industry was the talk of the
season. (Needless to say.)

LE SCANDALE

"Fine old French cognac and passion fruit juices! Together? It was a *scandale!*

"But, *mes amis,* this — Alizé — has become the rage.

"They've put just the right amount of smooth cognac into the tangy passion fruit juices. It makes a surprisingly good marriage. Refreshingly light.

"Henri likes Alizé on-the-rocks. Pierre likes his Alizé with a splash of soda. I love it with champagne. I call it Alizé Royale. *Magnifique.*"

Alizé
(Ah-lee-zay)
Now imported
from France.

Imported from France by Kobrand Corp., NY, NY., 16% alc. by vol.   Photo: Ken Nahoum

Eco

World

800-

e
mist

Weekly.

- 0 6 3 1

This campaign is a pure
distillation of **The Economist**
magazine and its editorial
product.
To define *The Economist*
in pragmatic, even descriptive,
terms would be impossible.
There are so many different
dimensions to this news weekly,
it would be a mistake to single
out individual features.
The campaign thus extends
straightforward, intelligent,
and clever lines indicative
of *The Economist*'s opinionated,
editorial tone, its global focus,
status, and its journalistic
integrity. The additional element
of intellectual humor creates
a sentiment of accessibility
since the reader is made privy
to the inside joke.
The color and typeface
of the ads is immediately
recognized as that of the
famous *Economist* masthead.
The absence of imagery and the
carefully chosen phrases also
serve to reflect the editorial
style and focus of this icon
of international journalism.

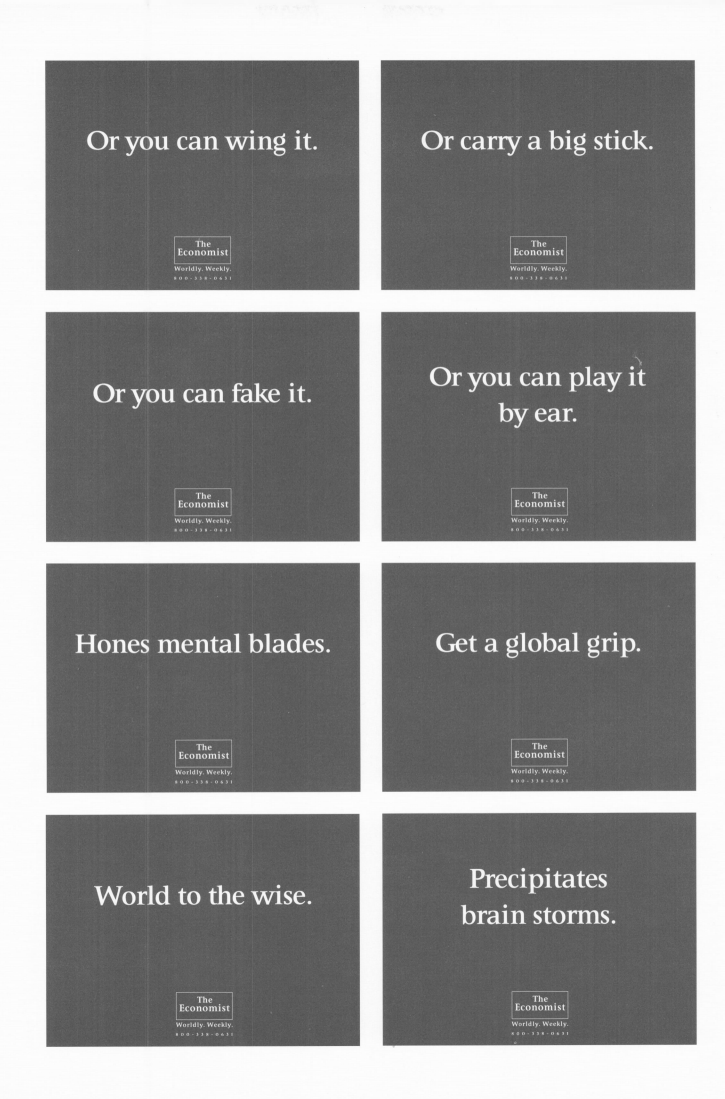

An offspring of the Hilton
International hotel chain,
Vista aimed to differentiate
itself by appealing to a younger,
more dynamic audience,
one that has the potential
to move from middle- to
upper-management circles.
The creation of this campaign
was contrary to the standard
process. Rather than using the
typical visual clichés to justify
why the hotel's services are
superior, images were chosen
for their singular dynamism;
to appeal to the fast-paced,
goal-oriented target audience.
Each image was then matched
with a projected situation,
a dynamic story with relevance
to the reader, to allow them
to imagine themselves in these
ultra-active situations.

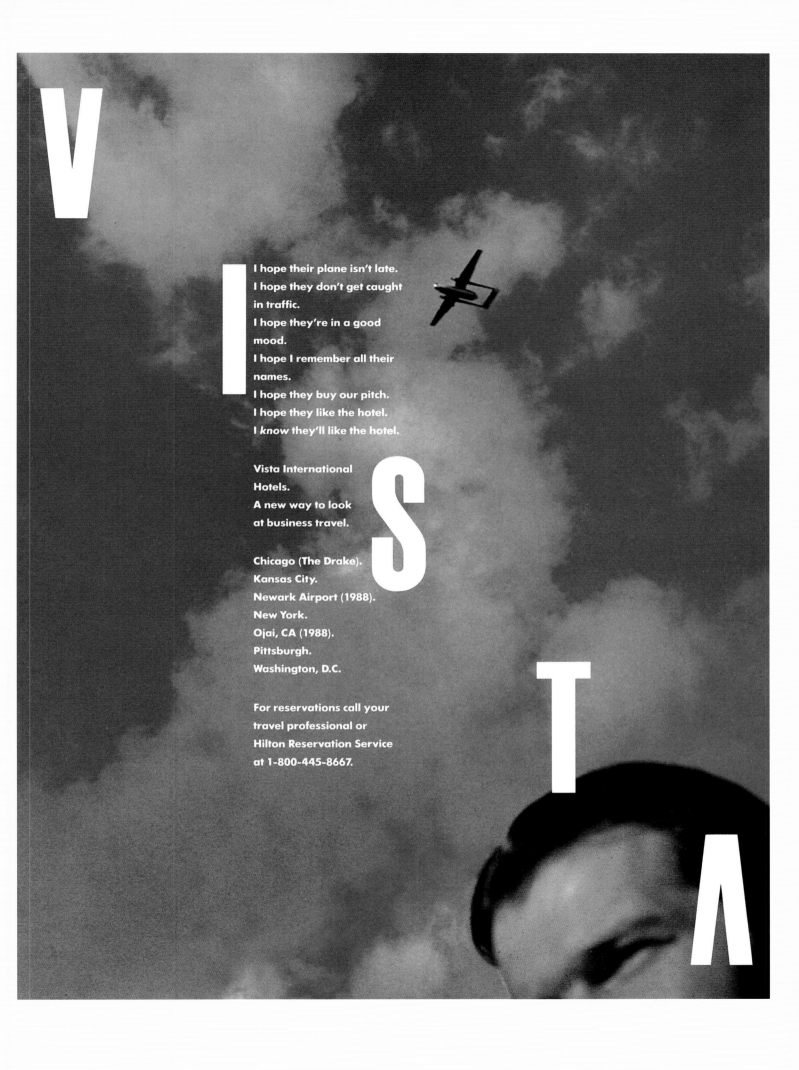

I hope their plane isn't late.
I hope they don't get caught in traffic.
I hope they're in a good mood.
I hope I remember all their names.
I hope they buy our pitch.
I hope they like the hotel.
I *know* they'll like the hotel.

Vista International Hotels.
A new way to look at business travel.

Chicago (The Drake).
Kansas City.
Newark Airport (1988).
New York.
Ojai, CA (1988).
Pittsburgh.
Washington, D.C.

For reservations call your travel professional or Hilton Reservation Service at 1-800-445-8667.

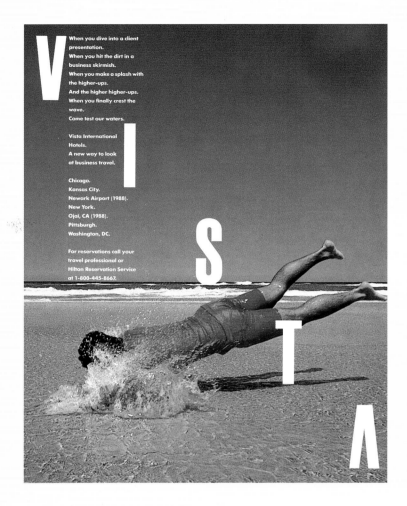

When you dive into a client
presentation.
When you hit the dirt in a
business skirmish.
When you make a splash with
the higher-ups.
And the higher higher-ups.
When you finally crest the
wave.
Come test our waters.

Vista International
Hotels.
A new way to look
at business travel.

Chicago.
Kansas City.
Newark Airport (1988).
New York.
Ojai, CA (1988).
Pittsburgh.
Washington, DC.

For reservations call your
travel professional or
Hilton Reservation Service
at 1-800-445-8667.

The long, low ride.
The calculated risk.
The smooth drink.
The smart suit.
The right hotel.
Rest for success.

Vista International Hotels.
A new way to look at
business travel.

Chicago (The Drake).
Kansas City.
Newark Airport (1988).
New York.
Ojai, CA (1988).
Pittsburgh.
Washington, D.C.

For reservations
call your travel
professional or
Hilton
Reservation
Service at
1-800-445-8667.

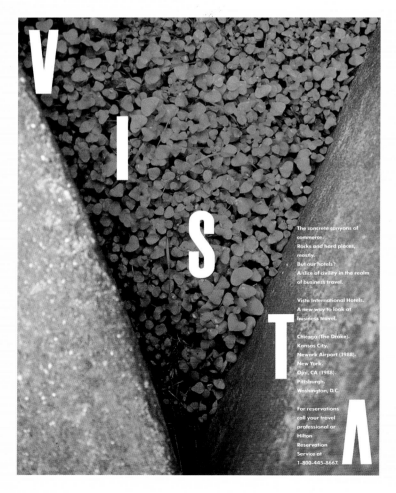

The concrete canyons of
commerce.
Rocks and hard places,
mostly.
But our hotels?
A slice of civility in the realm
of business travel.

Vista International Hotels.
A new way to look at
business travel.

Chicago (The Drake).
Kansas City.
Newark Airport (1988).
New York.
Ojai, CA (1988).
Pittsburgh.
Washington, D.C.

For reservations
call your travel
professional or
Hilton
Reservation
Service at
1-800-445-8667.

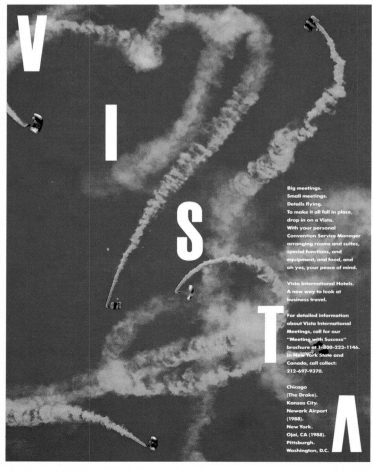

Big meetings.
Small meetings.
Details flying.
To make it all fall in place,
drop in on a Vista.
With your personal
Convention Service Manager
arranging rooms and suites,
special functions, and
equipment, and food, and
oh yes, your peace of mind.

Vista International Hotels.
A new way to look at
business travel.

For detailed information
about Vista International
Meetings, call for our
"Meeting with Success"
brochure at 1-800-223-1146.
In New York State and
Canada, call collect:
212-697-9370.

Chicago
(The Drake).
Kansas City.
Newark Airport
(1988).
New York.
Ojai, CA (1988).
Pittsburgh.
Washington, D.C.

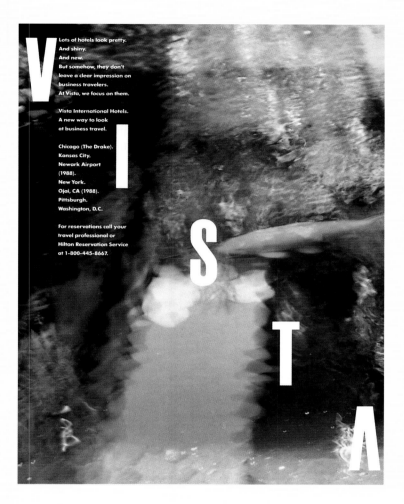
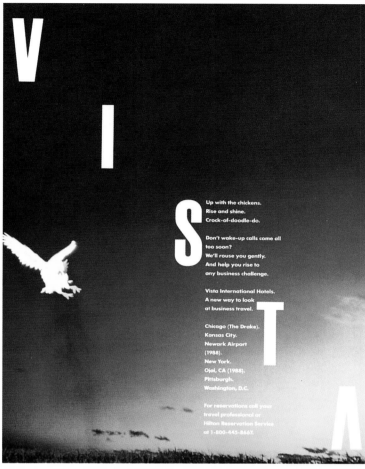
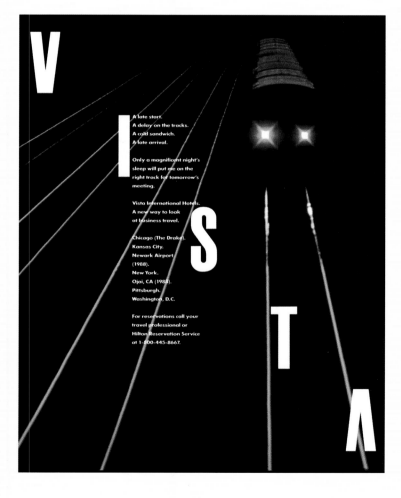

The **Kahala Hilton** is the
flagship hotel of the Hilton
International Properties.
Because of its exotic location
and unsurpassed standards
of luxury and service,
the Kahala is the kind of hotel
that has to be experienced
to be appreciated.
The ads from this campaign
convey the Kahala experience
by depicting the mysterious,
romantic, and lush environment
of the location, as well as by the
suggestion that a stay at the
Kahala will be the realization
of a dream come true.
The imagery in these ads
creates subliminal expectations
more valuable than any
pragmatic argument
about service.
The copy, which reinforces the
visuals, recalls an exotic,
faraway life that resonates
with the elite aspirations of
the target audience.

When I was a child, my nanny would read me stories like Treasure Island and Swiss Family Robinson. And I fell in love with the idea of shipwrecks and pirates and deserted islands in the sun.

So every time my husband and I come to the Kahala, the chef packs us an amazing feast and we sail the hotel's boat to the Kahala's tiny, private jewel of an island just offshore.

With my scarf as a blanket, we doze in the sun, recite what bits of poetry we can still snatch from our memories. And when we leave our deserted isle, we arrive at the hotel in time for some of the western world's most civilized dining and dancing.

That's the secret of the Kahala legend—the best of both worlds in a perfect setting. Nanny said you couldn't have your cake and eat in too. But Nanny was wrong.

Uncover the secrets of

the Kahala.

For information and reservations at The Kahala Hilton, Honolulu, Hawaii, call your travel professional or Hilton Reservation Service: 1-800-HILTONS.

Kahala Hilton

Fly uncrowded. Land unruffled.

While most airlines have followed the trend of adding seats, Swissair has not. For the simple reason that crowding makes for ruffled feathers.

Swissair 747's have 9 seats across instead of the usual 10; DC-10's, 8 across instead of 9.

Because widebodied aircraft should not only seat more; they should also seat more comfortably.

Ours do.

So our passengers have more elbow room, our flight attendants have more room to serve, and everyone is happier.

It shows, too.

Swissair has earned the greatest percentage of repeat business from experienced travelers.

They flock to Swissair, where comfort is the bottom line.

P.S. For those who really want to stretch out in peaceful slumber, Swissair 747's now feature a number of Slumberette seats in first class.

Swissair has worldwide departures from New York, Boston, Chicago, Montreal and Toronto.

Call Swissair or your travel expert.

This campaign is an excellent
illustration of how to
combine brand image and
specific product attributes
in a single message.
By announcing its redesigned
logo and aircraft look,
Swissair sought to reinforce
its name as a premier brand,
recognized worldwide for its
commitment to the highest
standards of service.
Several major themes are
emphasized throughout the
campaign: the newly designed
logo; the breadth and depth of
the fleet; the extension of the
worldwide network; recognition
of the need for comfortable
seating; and the unsurpassed
quality of the food and service.
Each of these themes is
presented with a bold visual
treatment. The birds sitting on
the "bottom line," for example,
demonstrate Swissair's
comfortable seating
configuration versus that
of the competition.

The word gets around.

Swissair has earned the greatest percentage of repeat business from the experienced traveler.

Demanding, experienced travelers who prefer to give Swissair their business.

Again and again.

Because they're accustomed to looking for the maximum return on their investment. Whether they are traveling for business or for pleasure.

It's just good business.

It's good business for Swissair too.

Swissair believes that in order to get the best, first one must give it. So we offer the best we can.

At no extra cost.

The best food. The best service. The best timetable.

No matter who you are. Or which class you fly. Our passengers call it Swiss Class.

It makes for many happy returns.

Apparently, word gets around.

Swissair has worldwide departures to 88 cities in 61 countries from New York, Boston, Chicago, Montreal and Toronto.

Call Swissair or your travel expert.

Only the cream of the crop flies.

Our chefs buy only the freshest and most expensive ingredients for our kitchens.

Anywhere.

Because they believe that good food really is the way to a person's heart.

Obviously, there are many who would agree. In fact, experienced travelers have rewarded Swissair with the greatest percentage of repeat business.

Which is not something we take lightly.

Because travelers who fly more, expect more.

So our chefs prepare five gourmet selections for every flight. Plus any one of 15 different special meals on request:

Hindu, Kosher, Moslem, diabetic, salt-free, vegetarian, dietetic . . . you name it.

Only the best will please Swissair passengers.

The cream of the crop.

Swissair has worldwide departures from New York, Boston, Chicago, Montreal and Toronto.

Call Swissair or your travel expert.

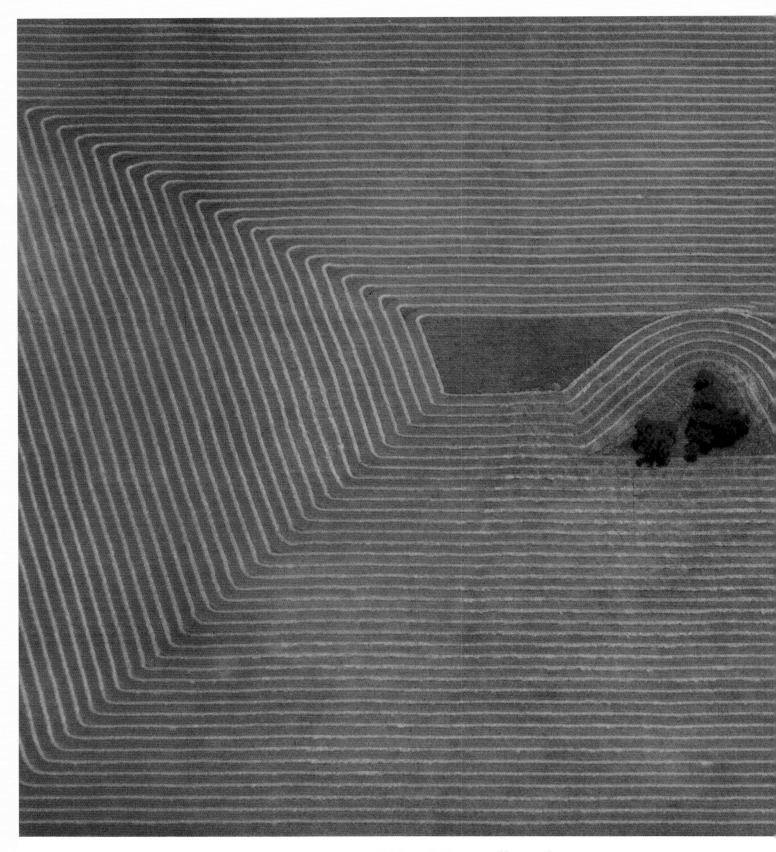

From our worldwide collection.

This view can be seen when Swissair Flight 142 passes over the summer harvest in the Pampas of Argentina.

However, Swissair also has hundreds of other views on view every week en route to 93 cities in 63 countries around the world. Each one serves as an interesting analogy as to why Swissair has grown to

encompass an international network of more than 173,000 miles. Because from up above, patterns may differ, but travelers everywhere are united in their demand for service.

Particularly experienced travelers.

Experienced travelers expect their airline to be efficient, punctual and consistent. Which explains

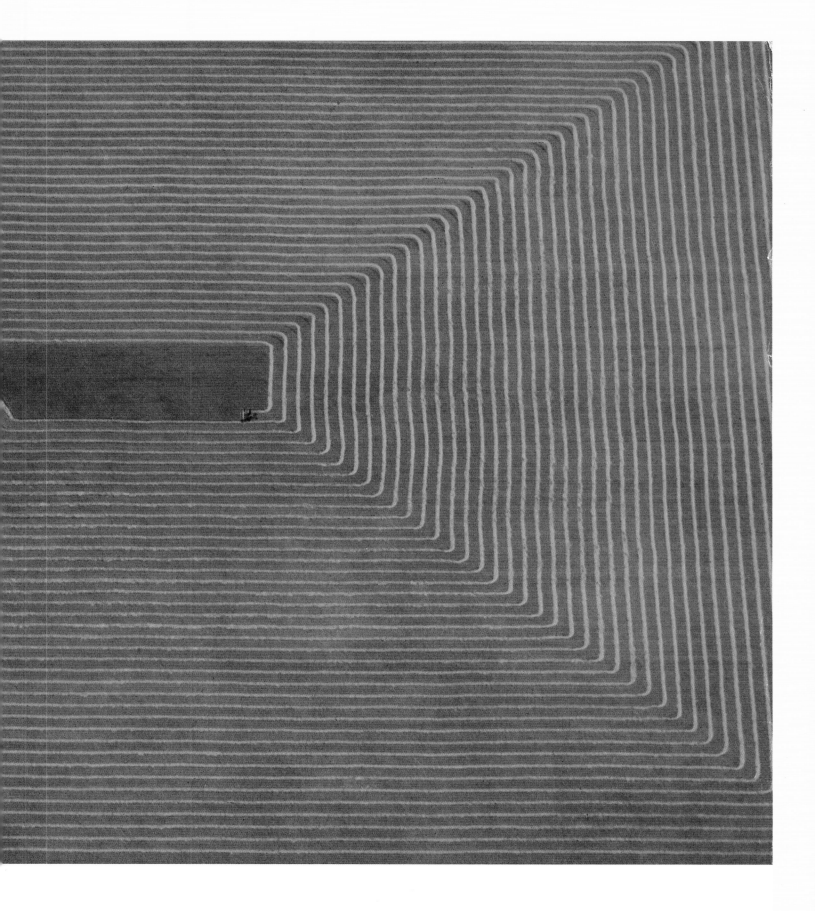

hy they give Swissair a greater percentage of their
usiness. They view service as an art.

And the art of service knows no boundaries.

Swissair departs from New York, Boston,
hicago, Toronto and Montreal to Europe,
en on to Africa, the Middle East, the Far East
d South America.

Call Swissair or your travel expert.

Ermenegildo Zegna

NEW YORK · COSTA MESA
ULTIMO · LOUIS · NEIMAN MARCUS · WILKES BASHFORD · M.PENNER

Ermenegildo Zegna

NEW YORK • COSTA MESA
ULTIMO • LOUIS • NEIMAN MARCUS • WILKES BASHFORD • M.PENNER

Ermenegildo Zegna is one
of the most revered Italian
fashion houses for men, known
especially for its fine fabrics.
However, this reputation
was also a well-kept secret – not
unusual for a manufacturing
driven brand. The challenge
was to create an approach
that would cut through
the clutter of ordinary fashion
advertising, and to extend
the positioning, which would
do justice to the superior quality
of the product and its classic
customer profile: men who "are
at home anywhere in the world."
By interjecting a Zegna suit into
a row of "professional uniforms,"
the ultimate utilitarian dress,
a striking juxtaposition
is created. It's easy to imagine
how this visual device can
be perpetuated. Zegna literally
stands out. A fact not lost to the
man (and woman) to whom the
advertising was directed. They
came, and predictably, stayed.

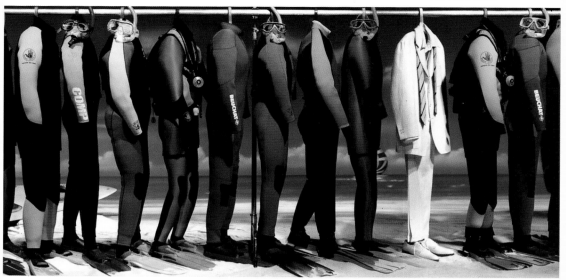

The man passes.

Time passes.

The dog passes.

Elsewhere, on a runway, a plane lands...time passes...another plane lands...or takes off. Repeat this, as Swissair does, in more than 110 cities in 70 countries. Repeat it like clockwork, mile after mile. And every mile adds up to bonuses for our frequent flyers. Go make your time count. For reservations and information regarding our Qualiflyer program, call your travel agent or Swissair. Time is everything.

"Sequence II"
by Harald Mante.
Part of Swissair's
Time & Motion
Series.

An exhibit.

How does one sum up the way
an efficient airline is run?
By guaranteeing passengers
a higher frequency of on-time
arrivals and departures,
as well as an assurance that they
will always enjoy the highest
standards of service. In short,
by managing a perfect balance
between time and motion.
To illustrate this concept for
Swissair, an extraordinary
campaign was developed
in collaboration with the
prestigious International
Center for Photography.
Through the Center, which
maintains the most famous
collection of works by history's
greatest photographers,
Swissair commissioned
the *Time and Motion* exhibition
featuring interpretations of time
and motion as seen through
the eyes of many well-known
photographers.
Swissair, as a result, became
associated with the touching,
humanistic images and themes.
The gesture of supporting
the arts also reinforced the
airline's image of leadership
and creativity in the industry.
The campaign, placed
internationally, was accompanied
by an extensive public relations
and direct marketing effort.
The exhibition traveled
the world, merchandised by
the local Swissair offices.

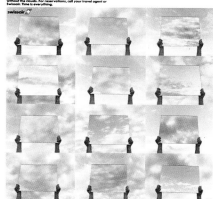

Minutes go by…you turn around, and years have passed. Time
gone. All the more reason to savor every moment and to make time
count. Swissair makes sure that the time spent is spent well indeed.
So you return relaxed and on time to the people you love. Swissair
comes and goes to 110 cities in 70 countries worldwide. For
reservations, call your travel agent or Swissair at 800-221-4750.
Swissair. Time is everything.™

swissair +

"Brothers"
by Art Rogers.
Part of Swissair's
Time & Motion
Series.

An exhibit.

Beauty should always speak for itself. Yet so much fashion advertising attempts to cover up the lack of style in both the product and its advertising through mundane verbiage and superfluous imagery.

In the case of **Via Spiga** of Milan, the customer benefit is exemplified by the product itself – the ultimate fashion statement.

The campaign showcases Via Spiga as a high-end, exclusive brand of shoe, by relying purely on the shoe's appearance and design for its presentation. The audacity of merely showing without telling, is further enhanced by the use of a single shoe rather than the pair, and by its placement on the soft folds of a luxurious fabric as if it were fine jewelry.

Finally, by simply using a color stat machine to produce the ad, the photograph takes on the effect of a painted still-life.

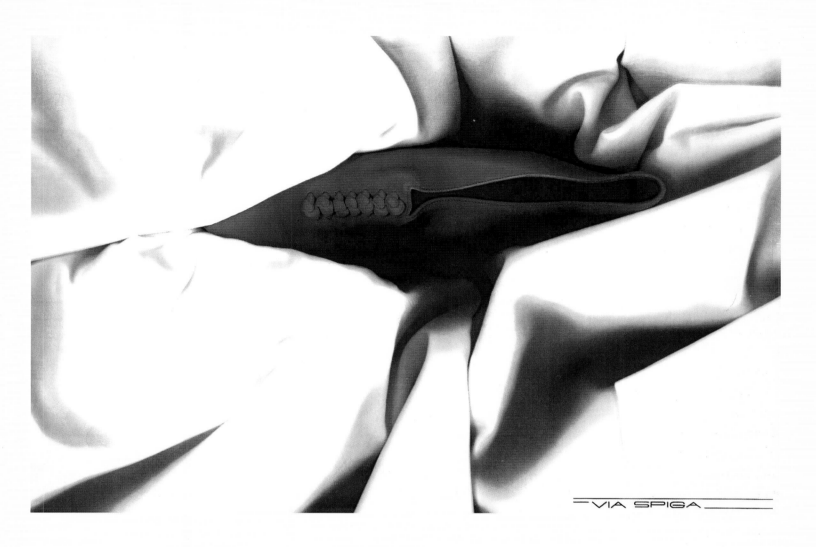

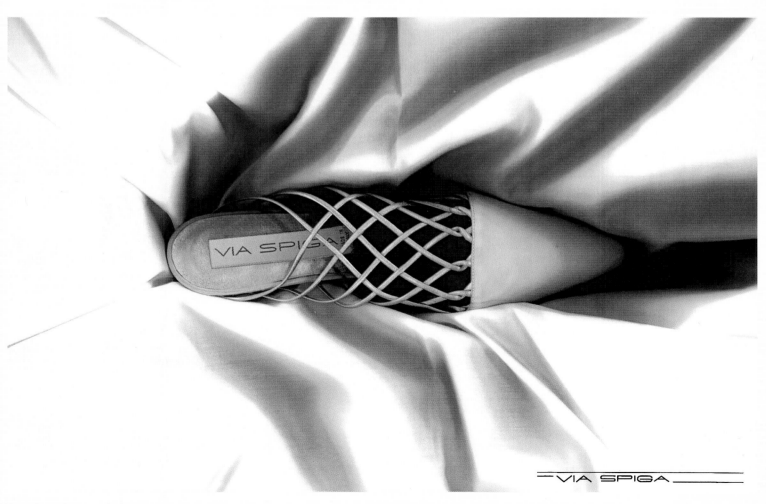

By reason of its long tradition of economic and political neutrality, Switzerland, and by association its airline, **Swissair**, has long been recognized as an independent entity. As the home of the European headquarters for the U.N., Switzerland is also regarded as an authoritative arbitrator and negotiator. This campaign brings together one Switzerland-based, global institution, the U.N., with another, Swissair, and presents them as partners for a good cause. Utilizing the U.N. as a formidable base, it was also possible to solicit the participation of celebrities as spokespeople for the campaign. Norman Mailer, Sophia Loren, Roger Moore, Hanna Schygulla, Jeremy Irons, and Geraldine Chaplin were just a few of the participants, and everyone who was approached donated their time and efforts to the cause. Swissair also benefitted from the campaign. The message contributed to the public's perception of Swissair as a force for the cultural and physical good of humankind, and as the "united nations" airline – truly global.

A
TRIBUTE
TO THE
UNITED
NATIONS

GBBS Photo: Michel Comte

"Over the past 50 years, the United Nations has led international efforts to provide humanitarian protection and assistance on a global scale. Its programs have assisted hundreds of millions of people."
Sophia Loren.

Sponsored by Swissair in cooperation with the United Nations Department of Public Information.

Swissair is ever ready to shorten the distance between people by transporting them to and from more than 115 destinations anywhere in the world. Time is everything.

Josie Natori, the accomplished fashion designer, managed to leverage her talent, energy, and limited budget by taking a gamble. She concentrated her entire year's media budget into a series of ads that ran in a single issue of the *New York Times Magazine*. This, along with a radically different visual approach, created the impression of Natori as an established force in the high-end lingerie business. In fact, reality followed perception, and the company achieved major brand status with leading retailers, to the extent that Natori was able to extend and license her lines. Of course, the culture of wearing lingerie has a rich history in the context of both the narcissistic and the sexual, and the surreal images of the ads play on these subliminal notions. Although there is a risk of appearing offensive, the controversy heightened awareness about the campaign. Courageous marketing decisions can create significant "pull" as well as provide the "push" that is often necessary to influence retailers to stock the product. It is an example of how to force the issue via the media.

A short cut, indeed.

NATORI
A STATE OF MIND

Air freight connects one
distant point on the globe
to another, extending the
physical and cultural conduit
through inches, centimeters,
pounds, and kilos.
Since cargo, on all continents,
is about size, the metaphor
of a measuring tape is obvious
and makes the point quickly.
The generic nature of cargo
service and **Swissair's**
favorable reputation made
a technical argument about
service redundant.

swissair + The yardstick by any measure.
Cargo

Baker is a high-end furniture
manufacturer that specializes
in reproductions of mainly
eighteenth-century designs.
Because the company
is committed to a manufacturing
policy of superior quality
and exclusive positioning,
it decided to break away from
the advertising typical of
their category.
The aim of the new campaign
is to take advantage of the
furniture-buying cycle of the
baby boom generation.
There are two significant
occasions in that cycle: when
the children are about to arrive,
and again when they
go off to college.
The strategy is to convince the
now older and more affluent
audience to invest in another
set of furniture – furniture of
extraordinary quality.
Here seen as an investment not
an indulgence, the furniture is
depicted as an heirloom
that will bridge generations.
This strategy appeals to
the common sense of the
audience, a far cry from
relying on the latest style and
price points.

Thank you for fixing my tie.

Now imagine this.

Imagine someday <u>his</u> grandson

doing the same.

Right where they're sitting now.

Baker
Furniture
Bridging Generations

Two birds of a feather,

with thoughts to share,

and the perfect nest

questions to ask,

in which to ponder the future.

Baker
Furniture
Bridging Generations

Swissair advertising is by
design very Swiss: high in
production value, well
strategized, and eloquent.
But it is also, perhaps, too
serious, too static, and lacking
in bite and humor.
This assumption was reinforced
by qualitative research which
indicated that Swissair, too,
was seen as very competent
and reliable, but not terribly
innovative or humorous.
The new campaign, then,
required a certain amount
of playfulness. It illustrates
all aspects of travel via
whimsical and dynamic
images, each a story in itself.
The campaign also mimics
the editorial style of the
lifestyle publications in
which the ads were placed,
and thus blended right into
the respective editorials.
Another feature of the campaign
was the high frequency of
insertion, which provided the
opportunity to cover many
aspects of the company's
services, while cumulatively
creating the impression
of changes in the corporate
spirit and attitude.

Peek-a-boo, we don't see you. Occasionally, frequent flyers neglect to claim their awards. Too bad, because our Qualiflyer program is as different as you are, and worth all your time in the sky. So please reveal yourself. Call now. Time is everything. swissair ✚

**A pragmatic approach to elegance.
Some people need all the room our First Class
provides. Others insist on a measure of
understated luxury. Our priority is the best
utilization of our passengers' time, so
we have no quarrel with either view. Time is**

An airline for mature travelers. Everyone knows about Swissair's outstanding service, superior food, and civilized terminals. Not everyone has discovered our fun-loving nature. It takes some time. Time is everything. swissair ✛

Swissair is a partner in the Delta, USAir and Air Canada frequent flyer programs.

Drop almost everything. Save effort. More important, save time. Leave your bags at any airport in the world. Pick them up at your convenience at any of 115 Swiss rail stations. Call now. Time is everything. swissair ✛

One should never judge an airline by its lobsters alone. There are other criteria, such as leaving and arriving on time. But if you insist on the crustacean yardstick, remember that bigger is not necessarily better. Time is everything. swissair ✛

Waltzing your way through the Swissair world. The Zurich and Geneva terminals make traveling to any of our more than 100 destinations in Europe, Africa, Asia and the Middle East like a classic Broadway musical. Effortless and timeless. Time is everything. swissair ✛

Swissair is a partner in the Delta, USAir and Air Canada frequent flyer programs.

Has our Business Class for Europe, introduced a year ago, truly revolutionized the standards of business travel? All we can say is that passenger surveys rate it the best there is. Our thanks to all our guests in the past and to all those who'll be jumping aboard in the future. Time is everything. swissair ✛

Leg room. Elbow room. Knee room. Room for your front and back. Room to unwind. Swissair's Business Class, on 747s and MD-11s, is a liberating experience. And when freedom's time arrives, there's no turning back. Time is everything. swissair ✛

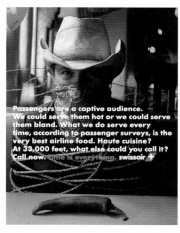

Passengers are a captive audience. We could serve them hot or we could serve them bland. What we do serve every time, according to passenger surveys, is the very best airline food. Haute cuisine? At 33,000 feet, what else could you call it? Call now. Time is everything. swissair ✛

Gravity and other laws. How do bumblebees fly when aerodynamics insist that they can't? They fly because they want to. That's our way, too. Every time we fly, to 110 destinations all over the world. It's a good way to run an airline. Call now. Time is everything. swissair ✛

Seeing the light. If we get to borrow the sky, we should at least take good care of it. That's why we fly a young fleet of planes, with clean, fuel-efficient engines, and recycle many items others throw away. Preserving our environment – an idea whose time has come. Time is everything. swissair ✛

Think of the great time you can have in the back of a Swissair plane. More than average room. Much better than average food. Well above average attitude. Economy Class it may be, but an average time in the sky it's not. Time is everything. swissair ✛

Maintenance is next to godliness. Clean is good. Neatness counts. So does common sense. That's why our fleet is among the youngest, cleanest, most fuel-efficient in the sky. We want you to be comfortable in both body and mind. Call now. Time is everything. swissair ✛

Is this an oasis in North Africa? Torrential waterfalls in South America or the Great Wall of China? If this is your Fata Morgana take Swissair for real. Swissair, flying to more than 110 destinations worldwide, takes you there in no time. Time is everything. swissair ✛

Flying big in a small world. Since you can only fly in one plane at a time, an airline's size doesn't matter. What matters is how well it takes you where you want to go and when. And that your time is well spent. By that measure, Swissair is very big indeed. Time is everything. swissair ✛

Changing planes in Zurich or Geneva is just a hop, skip and a jump for you and us. Which means you're up and down, in and out in almost no time at all. Time is everything. swissair ✛

"Of course Daddy will be here in time to tuck you in." He's coming home on Swissair. So he'll be relaxed, well-fed and happy to see his happy girl. That's time well spent in the air and on the ground. Time is everything. swissair ✛

Something's going on in Swissair's Business Class for Europe. Either you're getting smaller or the seats are getting larger. Anyway, you'll be spending your time in the sky sitting pretty. Time is everything. swissair ✛

In our new First Class World, the time has come to celebrate the fine art of timing: eat, drink, listen, work, watch, sleep – as often, as much, as little, as long and whenever you feel like it. Timing... sorry, time is everything. swissair +

Eating before you fly is usually a good idea. But on Swissair, where survey after survey rates our food as the best, it's not just a bad idea. It's a downright waste of time. Time is everything. swissair ✚

This campaign demonstrates that
extensive explanations are not
always necessary to sell complex
products or services – in this
case the benefits of **RAM**
wireless data communications.
By choosing vertical market
applications, both the bottom line
as well as the everyday, human
benefits of the service are
simultaneously and instantly
communicated.
In addition, the dramatic, spur-of-
the-moment photography
suggests immediacy and
practical application – both
crucial product features.

This campaign presents the
Swissair timetable and its
destinations from A to Z.
Reflected in both the content
and the design, the aim here is
to communicate the priorities of
the airline concerning care and
attention to detail – down
to the letter.
The frequent appearance of the
ads in the media also
reinforced the claim that the
sponsor indeed covers the
world from A to Z .

The function of print in daily
newspapers is instant
communication – "instant"
being paramount. This ad for
Swissair served as a news
report about the long-awaited
snowfall in the Alps. It is an
idea created, approved,
and implemented on the spur-of-
the-moment; placed overnight
to run the following day.
Here, one does not have the
luxury to search for that perfect
photographic metaphor; the
creative process must go
into high gear.
Good news. The phone
jumped off the hook.

It's snowing, It's snowing,

It's snowing in the Alps, it's snowing in the Alps. And it keeps coming down. This is the winter you've been waiting for. Ski packages starting at $293 for land costs • Guaranteed in U.S. dollars • Free brochure, The Alpine Experience™ • For information and reservations on 16 resorts and more • Call the Snowline at (800) 424-3424.

The world's greatest ski lift™. swissair

A new business magazine is
launched: **Manhattan Inc**.
The campaign is intended
to be a reflection of the
entrepreneurial lifestyle, and to
introduce the magazine as an
essential source for inside
information from the
powerhouse, Manhattan.
The ad mirrors the potential
readers' perception of
themselves as driven, smart,
street-wise, and having what it
takes to make it in the toughest
city in the world. The ad,
like the magazine, projects
the "whatever-it-takes"
excitement of doing business
in Manhattan.

The Business of New York
Manhattan, inc.

Whatever it takes.

If Manhattan had a motto, this would be it. Because Business in this town is all-out, full-power. Rule-maker. Rule-breaker.

Which also describes our new magazine. We're Manhattan,inc., coming in September.

An unabashed new business magazine devoted to telling the unvarnished, untarnished truth about what goes on here at the world center of Finance. Banking. Publishing. Law. Real Estate. Retailing. Advertising. Fashion. Entertainment. The Arts.

Written by Insiders. For Insiders.

And we'll make this promise. When there's a story to be told, we'll tell it. Come hell or high water.

For the rest of the story, call Joel Kessler, advertising director, 697-2100.

Swissôtel, an unknown commodity in Atlanta, introduced itself by means of two classic images: the crossbow, associated with Swiss folklore legend, William Tell, and the Georgia peach, positioned in the ad to be perceived as a substitution for the apple in the Tell story. This served to remind the readers that both regions are still steeped in tradition and customs such as story-telling and hospitality. By positioning the ads between the columns of the *Atlanta Journal*, the layout takes advantage of the paper's format, utilizing the well-read stock tables as an aesthetic element to separate the crossbow and the peach. This causes the ad to appear to be a double-page spread; in reality, of course, it is only two half-pages – a device also very appealing to the client's comptroller.

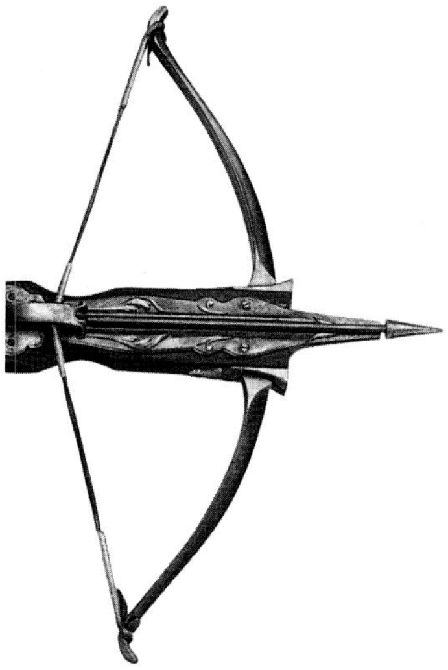

Mutual funds

Prices at which securities could be sold (net asset value) or bought (value plus sales charge) and change in selling price.

Fund	Sell	Buy	Chg
[illegible]	[illegible]	[illegible]	[illegible]

See MUTUALS, Page D7

Mutuals from D6

Fund	Sell	Buy	Chg
[illegible]	[illegible]	[illegible]	[illegible]

E—Ex capital gains distribution. s—Stock dividend or split. x—Ex cash dividend. f—Previous day's quotation. (NL)n—No front end load or contingent deferred sales load. p—Fund assets are used to pay for distribution costs-12(b)(1) plan. r—Redemption fee or contingent deferred sales load may apply. t—Both p and r.

Paper reveals some terms of Bass settlement

The Associated Press

ST. PETERSBURG, Fla. — After settling a shareholder suit with Texas billionaire Robert M. Bass and others, the Times Publishing Co. has emerged with $8.1 million in cash and a healthy balance sheet, newly disclosed documents show.

The company publishes the St. Petersburg Times as well as Georgia Trend magazine.

The settlement reached last August over the payment of dividends specified that neither side would reveal any details. However, Times Publishing has released some data to satisfy requests from the state of Florida.

The company agreed to buy back a 40 percent stake owned by the Bass group. The group had purchased the stake in August 1988 for about $28 million and had offered to buy the rest of the company for $270 million earlier this year.

Money and Interest

Interest rates

[illegible]

Gold prices

[illegible]

Silver prices

[illegible]

Foreign exchange

New York rates. Foreign currency in dollars followed by dollar in foreign currency.

	Yster-day	Prev day	Yster-day	Prev day
[illegible]	[illegible]	[illegible]	[illegible]	[illegible]

Commodity Futures

Chicago Board of Trade

Future	Open	High	Low	Settle	Chg
[illegible]	[illegible]	[illegible]	[illegible]	[illegible]	[illegible]

Chicago Merc. Exchg.

[illegible]

Intl. Monetary Market

[illegible]

N.Y. Commodity Exchg.

[illegible]

N.Y. Mercantile Exchg.

[illegible]

N.Y. Cotton Exchange

[illegible]

N.Y. Coffee Exchange

[illegible]

Index futures

[illegible]

Swissair customers get
a refresher course in this
campaign: a reminder to the
reader that at Swissair,
passengers are treated like
expensive commodities,
wrapped up and cradled
in comfort. The analogy
of precious fruit demonstrates
simplicity, integrity, and
uncompromising care.
The repetition of the graphic
shapes creates a bold pattern
on the page and produces
a "wallpaper effect" when the
images look as if they are
expanding beyond the format
of the page or poster.
The campaign theme was
also extended into the daily
operation of the airline.
Real fruit was made available
on stands at boarding and
handed out during the flight.
The fruit motif was also used
as a decorative feature on the
in-flight crew's ties and scarves,
as well as in the duty-free stores.
This is an example of how
to roll out the nucleus of an idea
into diverse and unexpected
mediums to create greater
brand identification
through repetition.

The top standards in Europe in terms of comfort, service and style are defined by Swissair Business Class - for people who can tell the difference. Time is everything. swissair +

Although a high-quality product in its own right, **Rioja wines** suffered from lack of awareness, compared to the more famous wines of Bordeaux. And because Spanish wines are generally lower in price, they are mistakenly perceived as being of lesser quality. Therefore, the intent of this editorial-driven campaign is to take the high road by acting as a leader. Educational in tone, it shows the reader and would-be connoisseur how to judge a fine wine – the inference being that Rioja wines are on a par with the best. Here is an example of how repositioning a product can enable the client to raise its prices, which in turn helps increase the perception of the product. Of course, the prerequisite for such a move is that the product is indeed of superior quality. The result: greater perceived value for the customer, more yield for the client. As a visual bonus, the placement of the two bottles creates a silhouetted shape of a wine glass in between. Some recognize it, some see it subconsciously. Regardless, the highly styled "advertorial" exudes authority – a prerequisite for a product that seeks more market share.

HOW TO LABEL
YOURSELF A
CONNOISSEUR

Ten years ago, if you overheard a comment like, "A robust body with an excellent finish, but overall a bit naive," you might have thought you were eavesdropping on a conversation about someone's mistress. Now, you recognize this as your cue to chime right in with your own observations on the latest well-reviewed vintage.

But unless your birth certificate includes such proper nouns as Rothschild, Loire or Napa Valley, how do you begin to acquire connoisseur status? Slosh your way through a pond of cuvées, quill poised over ever-ready wine journal? Memorize the wine list at some four-star restaurant until you know the glamour wines by heart? Nay, nay, nay.

The people who are responsible for the current wine phenomenon, the vintners from the Rioja region of Spain, think it's much simpler. Their rule of thumb? Choose a wine as you would choose a dear friend. Seek a depth of character from which new levels of interest may spring. Look for a gentle nature with enough complexity to make it captivating at parties and a delight at the dinner table.

On the following pages, we suggest a number of wines that can elevate you to cognoscente status. And label you a connoisseur. So toss aside that wine journal and pour a glass of wine from Rioja. To taste it is to love it.

Advertising only on billboards in the town of billboards, **Swissair** introduces its nonstop service to and from Los Angeles. As luck would have it, the abbreviation of Los Angeles, LA, can be found in many other words – including Switzerland – and the fun begins.

The clean and straightforward design stands out against the visual pollution along the freeway.

The campaign produced an impact that was larger than life, and Swissair's reputation was established in Los Angeles as the "civilized" alternative for the affluent traveler.

Civilization, coming to an airport near you.

The civilized way to the world. swissair ✚

Breathe Swissair.

The civilized way to the world. swissair ✚

To air is human to Swissair is divine.

The civilized way to the world. swissair ✚

On November 1st LA's air quality will improve dramatically.

The civilized way to the world. swissair ✚

Travelers usually associate
The Alps with Switzerland
and therefore don't think
of Germany, Austria,
Italy, and even Yugoslavia
as Alpine countries.
By making a creative play
on this geographic confusion,
the ad presents the Alps as
a country in itself. In addition,
it subtly links the entire region
with the common thread
of beauty. The text serves
to remind the reader
of the area's sophisticated
infrastructure, which lets
the traveler get around easily
and experience everything a
European vacation could
offer – in an area not larger
than the state of New Jersey.

Austriagermanyitalyswitzerlandyugoslavia.

It's the Alps. The resort where the best of five European countries comes together.

Austria, Germany, Italy, Switzerland and Yugoslavia have one tremendous thing in common — the Alps.

So it's only natural that part of each of these countries join to form the Alpine Region.

In the Alpine Region, everything you want out of a European vacation is in an area not much larger than New York State. It's the ideal resort for a vacation that knows no boundaries.

There's the music, the folklore, the festivals. The grandeur of baroque cathedrals, the quaintness of winding cobblestone streets. The spectacle of a sunrise over an Alpine summit and the quiet beauty of a sunset on a mountain lake.

For just a taste of how close everything is, consider this.

You could have breakfast in St. Moritz, lunch in Garmisch-Partenkirchen, break for coffee and strudel in Innsbruck, enjoy dinner in Cortina and top it all off with a nightcap in Bled — all in one day.

Better still, the dollar is strong in the Alpine Region right now. So you not only get fine quality, you get your money's worth.

This season, why settle for part of Europe when you can experience the heart of Europe?

The Alps. The European country that's one giant resort.

I'd like your guide to lead me through the Alpine Region. Please send me "Summer in the Alps."

Name _____

Address _____

City _____

State _____ Zip _____

Mail to: The Alpine Tourist Commission, 275 Madison Ave., 41st Floor, New York, N.Y. 10016

The most common impression
that people have of
Switzerland is an Alpine
country with rugged,
mountainous vistas.
Marketing research confirmed
this, as well as the fact that
neighboring countries enjoy
a better reputation for
attributes such as cuisine,
entertainment, and culture.
Thus, the campaign sets out to
educate the reader beyond this
narrow-minded perception of
the country. Using numerous
photographs (seventy in all)
assembled into an eight-page
"print video," it demonstrates
the unlimited variety
of interests and activities
available in Switzerland.
Each picture is numbered,
and readers are encouraged
to ask for further information
regarding its contents.
The whole point of the
campaign, to broaden
Switzerland's image,
is summed up in its tag line,
"Look no further, Switzerland."
The campaign creates
a valuable resource for direct
marketing, and the pragmatic
follow-up feature produces
tangible results.

41 45
42 46
43 47
44 48

17 21
18 22
19 23
20 24

25 29
26 30
27 31
28 32

33 37
34 38
35 39
36 40

9 13
10 14
11 15
12 16

49 53
50 54
51 55
52 56

60
57 61
58
59 62

Are you aware you have been looking at pictures of Switzerland? • The Alps and Landscape • The Cities, Villages and the People • Culture, Castles and Heritage • Ways to Travel and Places to Stay • Sports and Adventure • Foods and Wine • To learn more about Switzerland, fill in the attached card or call 1-800-GO-SWISS.

The Swiss National Tourist Office

Who better to get you to Switzerland than Swissair, with departures from ten North American gateways. And what better card to use to pay for your Swissair ticket than the American Express® Card. It's the perfect travel companion, welcome at fine establishments throughout Switzerland.

Don't leave home without it.®

L o o k   n o   f u r t h e r .   **Switzerland.**

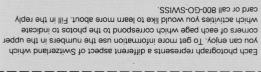

Each photograph represents a different aspect of Switzerland which you can enjoy. To get more information use the numbers in the upper corners of each page which correspond to the photos to indicate which activities you would like to learn more about. Fill in the reply card or call 800-GO-SWISS.

I would like to continue looking further.

Please send me information on the photos I have indicated

□ □ □ □ □ □

Name _____
Address _____
City _____ State _____ Zip _____
Telephone _____

AD 3/94

L o o k   n o   f u r t h e r .   **Switzerland.**

This ad for **Swissair**
celebrates Switzerland's
700th birthday. Type in its
most elementary application
serves as both the message
and the picture.
The reader first recognizes
the icon, the Swiss cross,
introducing the subject;
secondly, upon reading
the copy, the purpose and
announcement are revealed.

In 1291 A.D., in-
habitants of Swit-
zerland banded
together to fight
for a revolution-
ary concept called
independence. It
was an idea born
out of the notion
that Switzerland should be governed not just by the
people, but more importantly, for the people. And
they won. Now, 700 years later, those same principles
stand firmly in place. Which, perhaps, explains one
major characteristic of the Swiss populace – that after
700 years of working for the people, they would
inevitably become pretty good at it. Today, their national carrier, Swissair, takes that same spirit to over
110 destinations
within 67 countries
worldwide. Happy
700th birthday
Switzerland, and
many happy re-
turns. **Swissair.**
The civilized way
to the world.®

An ad in a newspaper
is by design short-lived.
Its appearance competes with
a fast-paced daily news
environment. So the mandate
for the creative strategy
and execution is to deliver
impact, long enough to get
the message across.
Creating the ad, one is faced
with a large, pristine, white
newspaper page. A playing
field for the distribution of the
verbal and visual metaphor.
That age old subliminal balance
between black and white.
A great challenge. The copy
in these **Swissair** campaigns
takes the lead talking about
a proprietary culture, as
it relates to the issues of
professional travel.
The visuals are the exclamation
marks. The featured ad is a
dramatic demonstration of an
approach, which only a company
with a solid brand equity can
take. A textbook example.

Everything you've heard about Swissair is true.

Swissair's First Class is legendary but, like most legends, descriptions fall short of the reality. We could tell you about the caviar and champagne, and what follows. We could tell you about the Slumberette seats that recline almost like beds. We could tell you about the service, so attentive to your needs. But telling you amounts to making claims...which just isn't first class. The real truth is...you simply have to experience it for yourself.

For information or reservations, call your travel agent or Swissair at 718-995-8400.

The civilized way to the world.®

Due to foreseen circumstances, this flight is on time.

It is said that the best insurance in business is preparation. You do it every day in your own business to stay on top of things. So, if you do it every day, you expect the same standards from everyone else. At Swissair, we anticipate everything that can possibly go wrong to make certain that everything will go right—whether it's before the journey, after, and every minute in between. As a result of these foreseen circumstances, you can plan on getting in on time.

All this staying on top of things is leading to another set of circumstances not unforeseen. For Swissair was recently voted tops by 9 of 10 frequent flyers.* But on-time performance shouldn't come as any great surprise. After all, we Swiss do have a bit of expertise in the area of keeping track of time.

On-time performance. Just another reason why at the end of the day, there is always Swissair.

*Source: December, 1991 issue of Airline Business magazine.

The civilized way to the world.®

swissair

Herzlichkeit... easier said than done.

In a recent survey, 9 of 10 frequent flyers told us that we're doing everything right*. Pleased as we are, that doesn't mean we can't do better. In fact, what we're continuously striving for is something much harder to achieve. It's called Herzlichkeit (pronounced Herts-leekh-kite). Translated, Herzlichkeit means genuine warmth and friendliness. The kind that can only come from the heart, and from the satisfaction of doing a job exceptionally well.

While our reputation for top notch service can be taken for granted, it's how we present it to you that makes it all come alive. That's Herzlichkeit. Of course, the next time you fly Swissair, we won't expect you to ask for Herzlichkeit, let alone pronounce it, but that's okay, we'll be doing our best to give it to you anyway.

Herzlichkeit. One more reason why frequent flyers know that at the end of the day, there is always Swissair.

*Source: December, 1991 issue of Airline Business magazine.

The civilized way to the world.®

swissair

A sitting ovation for the new Swissair Business Class.

So far, everybody who has tested our new 747 Business Class seat has given us a sitting ovation. That's because our new seats are simply the best. They are wider, have more leg room, recline further and have their own built-in leg rest. We also took one seat out of every row in Business Class. That means not only roomier seats, but more room in Business Class.

So the next time your business needs take you to Europe, make a seat-of-the pants decision and fly Swissair's new 747 Business Class.

And, by the way, all Swissair aircraft offer three classes of service to all of our destinations. Something most other airlines don't offer once they get you to Europe. Because once you get into Business, you'll want to stay in Business.

The civilized way to the world.®

This ad will put you to sleep.

At Swissair, we've noticed that seasoned business travelers want to have a quick bite as soon as they board, so they can get some sleep or finish up some work. Inspired by the challenge, our chef created the Quick Meal - a light, tasty feast that's every bit as good as our renowned cuisine, yet served when you want it and in one course. All you have to do is call and let us know ahead of time. Or, should you prefer the full feast, rest assured you'll be wined and dined slowly and plentifully - European style.

The next time you need to get some shut-eye on a business flight from New York to Zurich, call your corporate travel consultant, travel agent or Swissair at 718-995-8400 or 800-221-4750, board the plane, enjoy a delectable Quick Meal, and get some sleep.

The civilized way to the world.®

swissair

Where does the man who signs the checks check in?

If there's one thing that chairmen, presidents and comptrollers know very well, it's quality of goods or services received for money spent.

When it comes to air travel, Swissair always has represented the best return on investment a businessman can find, anywhere in the world. That's the reason why nearly 8 out of 10 Swissair passengers have flown with us more than once.

The attraction goes beyond money. As a matter of fact, on average, it doesn't cost any more or less to fly on Swissair than on any other airline.

The attraction has to do with the tangible extra services Swissair offers. For example, Swissair provides First Class on every flight, everywhere we go (most airlines don't).

The attraction also has to do with intangibles. For one thing, the genuine caring of Swissair flight attendants. For another, the attention to detail Swissair offers, and the consistency with which we offer it, not just across the Atlantic, but to 99 cities around the world.

Call us or your travel agent.

swissair ✚

Swissair treats everyone equally, more or less.

We learned long ago (1931 to be exact) that while cattle may not mind being treated like cattle, people definitely do. So we resolved to treat our passengers like people.

We also learned that while people come in all sizes, shapes and colors, they do not come in prices. In other words, we don't buy the affection of our First Class passengers at the expense of everyone else on the plane.

An example: we don't believe in serving good food in the front of the plane and not-so-good in the back. In First Class, you get more lobster because you've paid more money. In Economy, you get less lobster, but you still get lobster (or something equally wonderful) as an appetizer.

We have no "special section" in which we treat business people or anyone else "better than we used to," because we've always treated everyone exceptionally well.

In short, we did not get where we go (99 cities throughout the world) by being just another airline.

Call us or your travel agent.

swissair ✚

A salute to the real heroes of business travel.

Somebody had to go—you—and somebody had to stay—them.

Whether you're taking an important step up the corporate ladder or a routine business trip, they deserve some of the credit because they're paying some of the price.

You know what we mean. Missed dinners, missed Little League games, midnight phone calls, perhaps even extra days away from home. Despite all that, they're concerned that you're eating well, sleeping well and doing well.

That's why your wife wanted you to fly on Swissair. To her, Swissair represents an extension of home—not just one person to look after you, but a whole company of people whose very nature it is to take good care of other people.

Now, as you settle into your seat for the flight home, you remember that you forgot gifts for them. You'll find something from the duty-free shop on the plane.

You don't know it, of course, but having you fly on Swissair was really all she wanted.

Call us or your travel agent.

swissair ✚

This campaign for
Armenter Cigars provides
a case study for building a
premium brand in a hurry.
First, the features that classify
a great premium cigar are
discussed; then, the analogy
to the Armenter Cigar is made.
This strategy has the effect
of an advertorial where the
advertiser talks about the
subject generically, and
in so doing, becomes an
expert and spokesperson
for the entire industry.
Because the tone of the
campaign is educational and
informative, it appeals to the
many affluent newcomers who
are eager to learn.
By creating the notion of
Armenter Cigars as the
standard to which other
cigars should be compared,
an image transfer takes place,
and the new brand immediately
joins the more established
brands as an equal.
It is again important
to understand that before
embarking on such a strategy
one must be absolutely certain
that the product one advertises
is in fact of high quality.

BBC, the brand, is not only
known; it is revered, to the point
where the public sees the
corporation not as a commercial
venture, but as a cause.
This is enhanced by the
commonly held belief that
the BBC is government-owned.
Because of its heritage
of superior programming,
the BBC has a wealth of fine
programs available from
its extensive archives,
as well as many award-winning
contemporary shows.
Hence, the campaign's approach
to selling individual videotapes
by grouping them in eclectic
combinations and irreverently
stringing together the titles
of the programs, serves
to reinforce the awareness of
the BBC's impressive resources.
The effect is startlingly successful.
The headlines write themselves.
Their absurdity also evokes the
British sense of humor and, in
addition, offsets the staid,
serious image of the BBC.
Caveat: the series of featured
BBC ads were in development
at the time this book went
to press. The BBC campaign
has not been finalized and has
not been formally approved
by the client.

BBC VIDEO

Ad 1 (top left)

BBC VIDEO

All creatures great and small[1] trim trees,[2] in naked washington.[3] Absolutely fabulous![4]

 1 All Creatures Great & Small. Based on the world famous books of James Harriot, this immensely popular series deals with the trials and triumphs of a country vet. Set in the glorious Yorkshire Dales, it captures the simplicity and charm of pre-war rural England.

 2 Art and Practice of Gardening. For beginning and accomplished gardeners alike, this is a hands-on series that takes you through the steps necessary to create a great garden. It includes visits to famous British gardens and hints and tips from the experts.

 3 Naked Washington. From his earliest days in office, President Clinton has had a contentious relationship with the press-and this has been true of every president after JFK. M. Fitzwater hosts this documentary about power, the press, and the presidency.

 4 Absolutely Fabulous. Jennifer Saunders, Joanna Lumley. Follow the outrageous adventures of Patsy and Edina as they continue to live a life of excess and depravity through a non-stop series of hilarious adventures. Also available in a box set of four cassettes.

Now there's a place you can go for some of the worlds most Absolutely Fabulous video's. No it isn't a rental store or a pay-per-view cable channel. It's the BBC. Which isn't a name unknown for quality programming, or one you wouldn't expect to have dozens of Shakespearean productions. But would you also imagine thirty gardening video's. Lots and lots of cooking programs. Hundreds of educational and teaching video's. The worlds funniest collection of humour, including todays most talked about series, Absolutely Fabulous. Whatever you want, drama, science, history, we've got it. For more information on the entire collection, or to order. Call 1-800-BBC-VIDEO.

1-800 BBC-VIDEO.

Ad 2 (top right)

BBC VIDEO

Charles and Diana[1] at Fawlty towers[2] before falling on hard times[3] absolutely fabulous![4]

 1 Charles and Dianna. The first ten years of the stormy Royal marriage are chronicled in this fascinating video. Later events and developments make this record doubly poignant and significant as a historical record.

 2 Fawlty Towers. John Cleese, Prunella Scales. The unbelievably awful Basil Fawlty wreaks havoc in his resort hotel. The set includes: The Germans. The Psychiatrist. Kipper and the Corpse. Basil the Rat. 4 cassettes, slipcased.

 3 Hard Times. Dickens darkest novel is brought to magnificent life in this brilliantly acted production. Alan Bates as the pompous Bounderby and Richard E. Grant as the decadent Harthouse round out an all-star cast.

 4 Absolutely Fabulous. Jennifer Saunders, Joanna Lumley. Follow the outrageous adventures of Patsy and Edina as they continue to live a life of excess and depravity through a non-stop series of hilarious adventures. Also available in a box set of four cassettes.

Now there's a place you can go for some of the worlds most Absolutely Fabulous video's. No it isn't a rental store or a pay-per-view cable channel. It's the BBC. Which isn't a name unknown for quality programming, or one you wouldn't expect to have dozens of Shakespearean productions. But would you also imagine thirty gardening video's. Lots and lots of cooking programs. Hundreds of educational and teaching video's. The worlds funniest collection of humour, including todays most talked about series, Absolutely Fabulous. Whatever you want, drama, science, history, we've got it. For more information on the entire collection, or to order. Call 1-800-BBC-VIDEO.

1-800 BBC-VIDEO.

Ad 3 (bottom left)

BBC VIDEO

Churchill[1] cooking Hunan stir fry,[2] in a doll's house.[3] Absolutely fabulous![4]

 1 The Complete Churchill. This special edition collector's boxed set of four tapes presents the definitive story of the legendary statesman. Written and narrated by his official biographer, Martin Gilbert, it features never before seen footage.

 2 Far Eastern Cookery. A celebration of the myriad and distinctive flavors of the Far East, this video presents the favorite dishes of internationally famous chef, Madhur Jaffrey. The cuisine of Thailand, China, Japan, Vietnam, Malaysia and Korea is featured.

 3 A Doll's House. In the stifling society of the Victorian era, it was unthinkable for a woman not to be reconciled to her subservient role in society. Nora, a vivacious young mother refuses to accept this situation on Ibsens masterwork.

4 Absolutely Fabulous. Jennifer Saunders, Joanna Lumley. Follow the outrageous adventures of Patsy and Edina as they continue to live a life of excess and depravity through a non-stop series of hilarious adventures. Also available in a box set of four cassettes.

Now there's a place you can go for some of the worlds most Absolutely Fabulous video's. No it isn't a rental store or a pay-per-view cable channel. It's the BBC. Which isn't a name unknown for quality programming, or one you wouldn't expect to have dozens of Shakespearean productions. But would you also imagine thirty gardening video's. Lots and lots of cooking programs. Hundreds of educational and teaching video's. The worlds funniest collection of humour, including todays most talked about series, Absolutely Fabulous. Whatever you want, drama, science, history, we've got it. For more information on the entire collection, or to order. Call 1-800-BBC-VIDEO.

1-800 BBC-VIDEO.

Ad 4 (bottom right)

BBC VIDEO

Richard III[1] in an ornamental garden,[2] cooking chicken kiev.[3] Absolutely fabulous![4]

1 Richard III. Sir Laurence Olivier, Sir John Gielgud, Sir Ralph Richardson, Claire Bloom. Shakespeare's story of England's King Richard III, a desperate tyrant who seizes and holds on to the throne through a series of schemes and murders.

 2 Art and Practice of Gardening. For beginning and accomplished gardeners alike, this is a hands-on series that takes you through the steps necessary to create a great garden. It includes visits to famous British gardens and hints and tips from the experts.

3 World Cooking. Famous chefs from some of the world's most renoun restaurants discuss the preparation and serving of their favorite classical and regional dishes. Menu's and suitable accompanying wines are also covered.

4 Absolutely Fabulous. Jennifer Saunders, Joanna Lumley. Follow the outrageous adventures of Patsy and Edina as they continue to live a life of excess and depravity through a non-stop series of hilarious adventures. Also available in a box set of four cassettes.

Now there's a place you can go for some of the worlds most Absolutely Fabulous video's. No it isn't a rental store or a pay-per-view cable channel. It's the BBC. Which isn't a name unknown for quality programming, or one you wouldn't expect to have dozens of Shakespearean productions. But would you also imagine thirty gardening video's. Lots and lots of cooking programs. Hundreds of educational and teaching video's. The worlds funniest collection of humour, including todays most talked about series, Absolutely Fabulous. Whatever you want, drama, science, history, we've got it. For more information on the entire collection, or to order. Call 1-800-BBC-VIDEO.

1-800 BBC-VIDEO.

The awareness of **Austria**
is based on its historical
celebrities such as Freud,
Mahler, Mozart, and Strauss.
Although they are no longer
with us, their descendants
are, and through the portraits
and statements of Fraulein
Mozart, Herr Strauss,
Ms. Freud, Madame Mahler,
and others, the campaign
is thus seen as a cultural time
capsule come to life.
The portraits were taken by
the late fashion photographer,
Art Kane, and the copy
was written by Jim Durfee,
a member of the Advertising
Hall of Fame.
The campaign not only
activates the interest of
the potential customers,
it also resurrects the
traditional image of Austria
in the context of today.

Somewhere around 400 B.C., a group of Celts quit feuding long enough to build a little village on the Danube.

In 800 A.D. it was christened Vienna and that made everyone Viennese.

Which meant the search was on for some nice music to dance to.

When Johann Strauss, Eduard's great-great-grandfather, came along and gave us the waltz 1,000 years later, we lionized him.

But our national quirk, best expressed by the attitude that life is a stage to play on, compels us to go with the disco as well.

It's this love of all things pleasant that gives us Vienna with eleven stately concert halls on the one hand and 50 acres of lively amusement park on the other.

A sophisticated night life after the sun goes down, the quiet beauty of the Vienna Woods after the sun comes up.

It also gives us Innsbruck. An incredible ski center in the winter. An incredible vacation area in the summer.

And Salzburg, called "The Rome of the North." Except that doesn't do it justice.

And Graz. You've never been to Graz?

Or taken a river boat down the Danube? Or driven over the roof of the Alps? Or encountered a hot sausage at a "Würstelstand"?

It's time. And it's easy.

Swissair, the airline of the Alps and representing Austrian Airlines, is your logical choice.

Just give them a call or see your local travel agent.

Meanwhile, if you'd like to know more about the pleasures of our country, drop us a line and we'll mail you some beautiful things:

Austrian National Tourist Office, 545 Fifth Avenue, New York, N.Y. 10017.

"In Austria, our coffee houses remain faithfully old-world. I somehow wish the same were true of dancing."
Eduard Strauss

For as long as there has been a Vienna, there have been writers trying to put it into words.

Some gems out of the past include: "A never-ending festival of life." "A living museum of wonder." "Where the angels go on holiday."

And now Ms. Freud comes along with late 20th-century introspection and reminds us of the deeper aspects of Vienna's personality.

Which is not too surprising considering that Nicola's lineage includes great-grandfather Sigmund.

In the spirit of Ms. Freud's observation, could you ever again lift a glass of wine without a fleeting memory of an evening of music in an ancient wine cellar three stories below the city of Vienna?

Or not reflect on values as you study a line of youngsters camped out in an overnight wait for standing room tickets to an opera?

Or not realize you have an inner voice as something tells you, "why not..." as you join a table of Viennese at lunch. On pastries. Nothing but pastries.

However, we do hasten to point out that over 32,216 square miles of Austria are not in Vienna.

And there's so much variety and contrast throughout our country you'll be forced to make choices as with few other places in this world.

Which will also tell you something about yourself.

There's Salzburg, Innsbruck and Graz.

The Alps, the Danube, the steppes of Burgenland.

The music, the opera, the concerts, the festivals.

And a past that has merged into the present to provide all the amenities one expects in this modern world, yet all of the civilities one misses.

It's time. And it's easy.

Just see your travel agent, he/she will handle everything.

Meanwhile, we'd be happy to send you some enticing brochures on the "Jewel Box of Europe".

Drop us a line.

Austrian National Tourist Office 545 Fifth Ave., N.Y., N.Y. 10017 or 200 East Randolph Dr., Chicago, Ill. 60601 or 3440 Wilshire Blvd., Los Angeles, Cal. 90010.

"You'll know yourself better after Vienna."
Nicola Freud

Olivetti introduced its new
generation of word processors
at a time when more than
one competitor came out with
similar products.
Leveraging its Italian origin
and association, Olivetti
positioned itself as the ultimate
in style and industrial design.
The concept also plays
to the lifestyle aspirations
of the target user to influence
their selection at the moment
of purchase.

Olympia, a German typewriter
with a limited market share,
needed to build greater
brand awareness.
This campaign provides
a shortcut. By comparing
Olympia to another
well-respected German feat
of engineering, the BMW,
an image transfer is made.
Olympia thus gains instant
recognition and credibility
for its engineering and technical
savvy. Another ad depicts
the portable typewriter called
Carrera on (you guessed it)
the hood of a Porsche Carrera.™
While the featured technology
in this ad is now somewhat
dated, it nevertheless represents
an important example of a
classic image transfer.

Machine and Machine.

Yet another **Swissair**
campaign. The reader is drawn
in by the pure aesthetic
of the visuals. An oasis in the
clutter of magazine advertising.
It is designed to reflect
the relief the weary traveler
experiences when boarding
a Swissair airplane.
At the time of insertion
I was especially pleased by
a complimentary note from the
late Helmut Krone, the legend
and ultimate art director.

Swissair passengers can fly to 2 cities
in Switzerland. And 19 in Africa.

Swissair has never been a strictly
Swiss airline. But the service has never
been anything else.

Ask Swissair passengers who fly to
Africa. Many of them regard Swissair
as an African airline. Because we've
been doing business there for years.
Immersing ourselves in the culture.
Learning the customs. Understanding
the society's structure.

Then making it all work for Swissair
passengers. Of course, the food is a
continental success, on any continent.
The comfort assured. And those who
fly with us here get the same personal
attention they expect anywhere else
from Swissair.

But more than that, they have the
convenience of 48 different flights each
week to 19 cities throughout the
continent. On schedule.

To places like Casablanca, Abidjan,
Douala and Nairobi, which become as
familiar to our passengers as being in
Paris, London or New York.

Wherever they want to go, they
know Swissair is a natural part of the
landscape.

Swissair departs worldwide from
New York, Boston, Chicago, Toronto
and Montreal.

Call Swissair or your travel agent.

swissair

Swissair is a common sight in Africa.

Swissair passengers fly Swiss air
everywhere.

Swiss air is wherever Swissair
passengers are — all over the world. It's
in the skies of Tokyo, Buenos Aires,
Cairo, and 90 other cities in 63 countries.

Swissair is worldwide because there
are travelers all over the world who
demand consistent quality. Swissair
supplies it. Which is only natural.

Swissair is a Swiss company, and
Switzerland's greatest commodity is not
gold, but service. And service to the
Swiss goes beyond what the rest of
the world sees. For Swissair, the airline
of Switzerland, service is translated
into a promise.

A promise to get our passengers
from point A to point B with traditional
professionalism and expertise.

Consistently.

The experienced traveler has come to
expect it everywhere; in North America,
South America, Europe, Africa,
the Middle East and the Far East.

Board any Swissair flight, anywhere.
You'll see Swissair passengers have a
special air about them.

Swissair departs worldwide from
New York, Boston, Chicago, Toronto
and Montreal.

Call Swissair or your travel agent.

swissair

Swissair is everywhere — in the skies of 93 cities in 63 countries.

A crucial part of the creative
process is the give-and-take
between colleagues and friends.
Together, we have enjoyed
and suffered for that single,
hopefully brilliant, solution.
And here, I must stress, it is,
it must always be, a joint effort.
I have listed my many
collaborators, and I apologize
if I have missed someone.
There is one notable exception,
Juergen Dahlen, who not only
worked on many of the ads
in this book, but also played
a critical role in the concept,
art direction, and design.
It has been said that advertising
agencies deserve the clients
they have. If that's true,
I'm very fortunate, indeed.
Their collaboration and
understanding creates the
culture in which the creative
effort can flourish.
A hearty "thank you" to all.

Richard Avedon

Andrew Bettles

Gary Beydler

Rolf Bruderer

Chris Callis

Lou Cohen

Simon Hoi-Sang Chan

Michel Comte

Craig Cutler

Jim Durfee

Harold Edgerton

Robert Evans

Peter Fischer

William K. Geiger

Andy Goodwin

Danny Gonzalez

Timothy Greenfield-Sanders

Adriana Groisman

Ralph Halder

John Hamel

Frank Herholdt

George Holtz

Ken Josephson

Art Kane

David Katzenstein

Geof Kern

Karen Kuehn

Kazumi Kurigami

Rob Lang

Barry Lategan

Ann Lemon

Larry Levinson

Tom Mabley

John Manno

Claude Mougin

Hitoshi Nomura

George Parker

James Parry

Irving Penn

Rob van Petten

Rolf Preisig

Sydney Roach

Art Rogers

James Salzano

Bertel Schmitt

Sujeong Shin

Hermann Strittmatter

Joyce Tenneson

Jerry Tobias

John Turner

Nick Vedros

Frederique Veysset

Christian Vogt

Albert Watson

Claus Wickrath

Irene Wildbolz

Elena Zaharakos

Victor Zahn

Marcus Zimmerman